THE KINGDOM
OF GOD

VOLUME ONE

THE KINGDOM OF GOD

VOLUME ONE

THE FUTURE BREAKS IN

Tom A. Jones
Steve D. Brown

www.dpibooks.org

The Kingdom of God—Volume One
©2010 by DPI Books
5016 Spedale Court #331
Spring Hill, TN 37174

All Scripture quotations, unless indicated, are taken from
the NEW INTERNATIONAL VERSION.
Copyright ©1973, 1978, 1984 by the International Bible Society.
Used by permission of Zondervan Publishing House.
All rights reserved.

The "NIV" and "New International Version" trademarks
are registered in the United States Patent Trademark Office
by the International Bible Society.
Use of either trademarks requires the permission of
the International Bible Society.

Printed in the United States of America

Cover Design: Brian Branch

ISBN: 978-1-57782-257-8

To the evangelists and elders and their wives
of the Greater Nashville Church who have encouraged us
with their great openness to the life of the Kingdom.

CONTENTS

ACKNOWLEDGMENTS

*For prophecy never had its origin in the will of man,
but men spoke from God as they were carried along
by the Holy Spirit.*

2 Peter 1:21

In this passage Peter is acknowledging that men can't take credit for Scripture. They may have written it down and used their minds and hands to get it written, but ultimately it was God who was at work through any variety of circumstances, backgrounds and even problems to have it say what he wanted it to say.

In one sense the book you hold in your hand is not like this. It is not inspired Scripture and if the Bereans in Acts 17 studied to see if the things Paul said were true, you will need to do this all the more with what we write. But in another way this book is like the word Peter spoke of, particularly meaning that we as the authors *can't take credit for it.* Don't misunderstand; we do have to *take responsibility* for it. If it misrepresents biblical ideas, we can't blame anyone for this and rightfully should be taken to task.

But on the other hand, we must acknowledge that so many other people and so many other writings played a major role in shaping our thinking. In the interview that is included at the back of the book we mention especially many of these who have played a key role during our two years of intensive study of the concept of the Kingdom. When drawing on the works of others, we, of course, have tried to accurately give credit, but the endnotes will not reflect all the influences we are grateful for. We do want to single out two who were important in the final stages: Chuck Pike of Boston and Steve Staten of Chicago. They carefully read our manuscript and gave much helpful feedback. These men probably would have made more changes than those we made, but we know their help led to a better book.

We also must acknowledge the invaluable help of our most exceptional editor, Sheila Jones, who is that unusual person who is both a superb writer in her own right and also an excellent editor. An editor is the reader's advocate, and she does the job for all of you so well.

In the end we look to God, who works for our good in all things as he rules and reigns in his Kingdom, and we say,

For from him and through him and to him are all things.
To him be the glory forever! Amen.
Romans 11:36

Introduction

The Kingdom of God

THE FUTURE BREAKS IN

The message of so much popular Christianity is "Believe in Jesus, and get saved so you can go to heaven when you die." In this book and the two that will follow it, we will propose that Jesus' message is much better summed up with this idea: "The Kingdom of God is here. Let your life be transformed and live heaven's way right now on earth *and* in the age to come."

This book is for every person who believes it is crucial to seriously follow Jesus. It will be disturbing to anyone who is comfortable with cultural Christianity. This book is for leaders who want their churches to be shaped by the message of Jesus, even if that means radical changes. It will likely be an irritant to those who hold to historic evangelical positions that may bear little resemblance to the Sermon on the Mount.

This book is for seekers who still suspect that there is something about Jesus that traditional religion may have

1

missed. It will not be helpful to those wanting to shape their own spirituality in their own way on their own terms. Ultimately, this is for all those who are open to a whole new paradigm for living out God's will.

The Gospel of Mark tells us:

> After John was put in prison, Jesus went into Galilee, proclaiming the good news of God. "The time has come," he said. "The Kingdom of God is near. Repent and believe the good news!" (Mark 1:14–15)

The main theme of Jesus' preaching was "the Kingdom of God." On this, scholars, whether liberal or conservative, all seem to agree. The phrase occurs more than a hundred times in the four Gospels, and that includes the references to the "kingdom of heaven" in Matthew, which refers to the same thing but is worded differently.[1]

To say that the Kingdom of God was Jesus' main theme is to say that it should get the attention of all those who are serious about following him. And yet the concept has been plagued by misunderstandings. As we study more carefully Jesus' message in its Jewish context, we will see it was greatly misunderstood by the people of his day.

For roughly 250 years after Jesus, the church seemed to have a strong grip on the kingdom principles that Jesus taught. However, when we consider how the Roman Emperor Constantine turned his affections to the Christian faith, we may have questions about where his heart was, but we cannot doubt that his life and actions dramatically changed Christian thinking and practice. In his quest to become emperor reigning over the world's greatest kingdom, Constantine had to defeat another who was seeking the same goal. Of course, we don't mean he had to win an election but that his army had to win a bloody conflict. On the eve of a great battle at the Milvian Bridge, the future emperor, who had been exposed to Christianity by his mother, looked up to the sun and believed that he saw a cross of light above it, and with it the words "by this conquer." Constantine commanded his troops to adorn their shields with a Christian symbol (the letters Chi and Rho), and thereafter won the battle. He became one of the first of millions who would say their prayers in Jesus' name and go kill for a kingdom. How ironic that the sign he spoke of referred to one who told his disciples not to fight, and then laid down his life for his enemies. The new emperor ushered in a sea change in the understanding of the Kingdom that led to a distortion of its meaning that still profoundly affects millions of average believers.[2]

We are joining a chorus of other writers and teachers who are saying that it is time for us to throw off these distortions and listen afresh to Jesus' message. It will be our aim in this series to show that the concept of the Kingdom of God is central to Christian discipleship and an umbrella under which many key Christian ideas make sense and find their place. If there is anything we should pray to understand clearly, it is what Jesus meant when he talked about the Kingdom.

It is perhaps no exaggeration to say that when we begin to see our relationship with God through an understanding of the Kingdom, we will shift to a whole new paradigm for thinking about what it means to follow Jesus. Furthermore, we do not believe it is an exaggeration to say that a whole-hearted embrace of Jesus' gospel of the Kingdom could revolutionize our churches—bringing about a drastic change in spiritual culture even among those who are already serious about discipleship. But there are several other things we want to say by way of introduction.

1. One does not have to understand all we present to be in the Kingdom of God and to be living what we will call the kingdom life. Some will find that they have spoken about the Kingdom of God in wrong ways or have not understood some key concepts. Thankfully one need not have a master's degree in kingdom theology to be living in God's Kingdom. As we will see, Jesus said it was hidden from the wise and learned but revealed to little children. Anyone who has biblically responded to the gospel of Jesus and seeks to live his or her life under the Lordship of Jesus is a citizen of the Kingdom. That being said, it is always to our advantage to understand more fully and more correctly a biblical idea, and that is particularly true with such a crucial one as the Kingdom of God. The more accurately we understand God's plan, the better we are able to live it.

2. You may not immediately embrace every conclusion we have come to and, of course, that is not a problem. As we introduce what might be some new ways of thinking, we hope you will neither impulsively jump on board nor defensively react. What we are encouraging is that you have the heart found in the Bereans in Acts 17 and keep studying to see if these things are true. We do not think for a moment that we have our arms around the imposing idea of the Kingdom, and we are suspicious of anyone who thinks they do. We continue to learn, which means we must be open to changing our own minds. Of course, we always must be ready to bring our traditions and our feelings (both powerful influences) and lay them at the feet of Jesus. The gospel of the Kingdom will challenge them both in ways we may not yet have realized. There are some deep-rooted, but unbiblical, Christian reflexes that we often have to overcome.[3] We will need a radical openness to new understandings if we are to be the good soil that Jesus spoke of in one of his kingdom parables. We would hope that you read this volume more than once. You are probably like us, and miss a lot of things the first time through a book.

3. We should not be afraid. We say this because in the months when we were first engaged in deeper study of kingdom concepts, and shared a few of the insights with others, we sometimes heard expressions of fear. At times we were asked "Where is all this going?" Our answer, then, as well as now: We honestly don't know. We just want to go there if it means more fully being under God's rule and reign. To the best of our ability we are not going to call for one thing that we cannot find Jesus calling for. Some of what Jesus calls for *is* on the scary side. It is safe to say that the more deeply we go into kingdom teaching and living, the more we will become aliens and strangers in this world. That can give us pause. Perhaps what we should say is, "Don't let fear control you." Jesus is not going to beckon us to go some place without fulfilling his promise that he will be with us always.

4. We should act on what we become convinced of. The more we practice kingdom teaching, the more we will understand it. One of our concerns is that some people might read this and see it as argument for changing a doctrinal position and treat it just as an intellectual exercise. If there is anything that is clear about Jesus' teaching on the Kingdom, it is that it must be lived. And so to whatever extent you understand it, put that understanding into practice as soon as possible. Whatever you do, do something.

5. The more involvement you can have in talking through these ideas with others the better. As we will see, kingdom teaching was never meant to be practiced individually but in community. The very nature of the Kingdom requires this. To be reading, studying, questioning and concluding with others who are committed to encouraging the kingdom life represents the absolute best way. This book was born in an environment in which we were studying with others, talking, emailing and praying about what we were learning. We cannot imagine where we would be with this message were it not for the fellowship of people in our congregation with whom we have been able to share our journey.

6. All through this study, we must keep a clear view of God's grace. As we will see, the Kingdom itself comes as an act of God's grace. We enter the Kingdom as a result of God's grace. Jesus' gospel of the Kingdom and Paul's gospel of God's grace are the very same gospel. We will be transformed within the Kingdom because God continues to give grace to the poor in spirit and to the humble. We do not bring the Kingdom by our efforts, and we do not live the kingdom life by depending on our own moral power and human resources. To use the thought of Jesus in Matthew 6, we will live in a new way because of "the much more of the heavenly Father."

The kingdom message is a call to a new way of living that shows loyalty to another king, but it is made possible only because of the extravagant generosity of that king. If at some point the "good news of the Kingdom" does not sound like good news to us, it will likely be because we are focusing on some hard thing kingdom people are called to do and not focusing on the abundance of grace that God gives to those who hunger and thirst for righteousness.[4]

We likely will be asked why we are releasing this as three shorter volumes rather than one larger one. The answer is simple. We want as quickly as possible to encourage more Christians and churches to give thought to kingdom teaching and begin some serious discussion. Given our own limitations, getting all our material into print in one volume would simply take much longer. We are eager to share with you some of the most exciting, stimulating and challenging truths that we have found in our more than seventy-five combined years of seeking Jesus and studying his word.

In this volume we will look at the way the Kingdom was envisioned and anticipated during the Old Testament period and the clues that especially the prophets give us to its nature. Then we will turn to the heart of the book: Jesus' preaching of the good news of the Kingdom. While for us there are still mysteries of the Kingdom, we want to focus on what we can know about the Kingdom as Jesus announced it and proclaimed it. We will find there is quite a lot. After seeing that the Kingdom is here in Jesus, we will look at how it is to be lived in this world now by the church. A final chapter will examine the completed nature of the Kingdom that is yet to come in the form of a new heaven and a new earth, and how we are to faithfully wait for it.

In the projected *Volume Two: The Sermon and the Life*, which we mention being conscious of James 4:13ff and the tentative nature of man's plan, it is our goal to look at the Sermon on the Mount, which probably should be viewed as the Sermon on the Kingdom. As we will say later in this book, there is no section of Jesus' teaching that gives us a better look at kingdom life—a life, by the way, that he expects those who acknowledge him to live.

In *Volume Three: Aliens, Strangers and a Light to the Nations*," we will, God willing, more deeply delve into some of the issues raised in the first two volumes and even some new ones that some of our readers of the first two volumes will send our way.

We end this introduction with a prayer we will return to several times.

Our Father who is in heaven,
Let your name be revered.
Let your kingdom come.
Let your will be done on earth as it is in heaven.

Questions for Study and Discussion

1. Share or write down a brief statement describing what the idea of the Kingdom of God means to you.
2. How would you say the idea of the Kingdom has affected your thinking and the way you live?
3. Prior to reading this introduction, what would you have said was the main theme of Jesus' teaching?
4. What strikes you about the experience of Constantine before the battle at Milvian Bridge?
5. Read Matthew 16:16-23. How might Peter and Constantine have had the same misunderstanding about the nature of the Kingdom of God?
6. Some mistakenly think Jesus' message of the Kingdom and Paul's message of grace go in different directions and have little in common. Why is it essential to see grace clearly as you listen to the message of the Kingdom?
7. How open are you to new ideas? When is the last time you studied something carefully and changed your mind? Why might you resist some new perspectives on the message of the Kingdom?
8. What will help you make the decision to be open to new ways of thinking?

NOTE: We include discussion questions at the end of each chapter, but they are also available on the web with permission to print and copy. (kingdombooks-vol1.blogspot.com)

1

The Kingdom Is Coming

THE VISION OF THE KINGDOM IN THE OLD TESTAMENT

Early in his ministry, while delivering what is called the Sermon on the Mount, Jesus spoke these words: "Do not think that I have come to abolish the Law or the Prophets; I have not come to abolish them but to fulfill them" (Matthew 5:17). His reference, of course, is to the Old Testament Scriptures, and he is clear that he is not coming to show disrespect for them or to destroy them. Instead, his life and work represent continuity with those Scriptures, and he sees that his mission is to fulfill them or to complete them.

Marcion, a second-century writer named as a heretic by the church, taught that the God of the Old Testament and the God of the New Testament were different entities with completely different characteristics. His view was completely rejected by the majority of the church, and Jesus' statement in Matthew 5:17 would have been sufficient to support this judgment.

Having made this statement, Jesus then went on to perfectly fulfill all the goals, dreams, shadows, types and prophecies of the Old Testament. Jesus embodied the Israel that God had always wanted his people to be. As Paul wrote in 2 Corinthians 1:20, "For no matter how many promises God has made, they are 'Yes' in Christ. And so through him the 'Amen' is spoken by us to the glory of God."

Since Jesus fulfilled everything in the Law and Prophets (see also Luke 24:27), and since the inauguration of the Kingdom of God was his central message, we will surely find that the dream for the coming of this Kingdom was pointed to by the writers of the Old Testament. Thus, we will open our discussion of the Kingdom by examining material from the Hebrew Scriptures.

As we turn to these Scriptures, we must be candid about what we will not find and what we will find. We will not find that the idea of the Kingdom of God is fully developed and confronts us coming and going. We will find references to "his Kingdom" as in "The Lord has established his throne in heaven, and his kingdom rules over all" (Psalm 103:19). However, we will not actually find the phrase "Kingdom of God" at any point.[1]

However, here are some things we will find:

1. A pillar of Old Testament theology is the fact that God works in history, and then, it will only be logical to see that God was at work to bring history to

some conclusion in which his sovereignty would be clearly shown. Obvious evidence of this is found in the term "the day of Yahweh," heard often from the lips of the prophets.

2. A consistent message is that God has called a people to be his very own, and he has a plan for their life as a people—a plan for them to be a "light to the nations" (Isaiah 42:6, 49:6, 51:4).[2]

3. The only right relationship with God is one in which his kingly rule and reign is acknowledged.

4. At the same time we will see that God's will for his people remains unfulfilled usually because of their stubborn or wayward hearts.

5. These people he has chosen push their relationship with him to the very brink, but he continues to speak through his prophets concerning a new day when there will be a new covenant and a new way of being God's people.

6. God is going to bring his people back from their long exile and Yahweh (the Lord) himself will return to Zion where he will rule over his people (Isaiah 52:8).[3]

7. Throughout the Old Testament, God has dropped clues here and there that point to a vision or dream that God has for a people—from all nations—that will be under his rule in a special way.

8. And, finally, we will find people longing for the fulfillment of these promises and clues, even as they

often misunderstand them or view them through un-spiritual eyes.

A Kingdom of Priests

Very early in the story of the Jewish people comes one of those remarkable passages that buttresses one's faith in the inspiration of Scripture because it is so unlike what men would write on their own. In Exodus 19:3–6 God describes the vision he has for the people he is calling:

> Then Moses went up to God, and the Lord called to him from the mountain and said, "This is what you are to say to the house of Jacob and what you are to tell the people of Israel: 'You yourselves have seen what I did to Egypt, and how I carried you on eagles' wings and brought you to myself. Now if you obey me fully and keep my covenant, then out of all nations you will be my treasured possession. Although the whole earth is mine, you will be for me *a kingdom of priests* and a holy nation.' These are the words you are to speak to the Israelites." (emphasis added)

Shortly, God will call Moses to the top of Mount Sinai and give him the commandments on tablets of stone, but two days before this he is giving his people a vision of what he wants in their relationship with him and the kind of people he wants them to be. We see it as no coincidence that this comes before he gives them the commands. Biblically, it is sound principle to first talk of character and then talk of rules or commands. And so he tells them:

- He acted in their behalf to bring them to himself.
- He wants their obedience and loyalty (in other words, to be their king).
- But unlike what we find with the pagan gods, he wants a relationship with the people in which he shows them concern and affection.
- The relationship is conditional. God is the primary actor, but they would have to respond, obeying and keeping the covenant.
- "You will be for me a kingdom of priests and a holy nation."

It is this last phrase that is most striking. At a time when every nation would have preferred to have a kingdom of warriors, Yahweh wants his holy nation to be a kingdom of priests. The whole idea of the priesthood is fairly undefined at this point. Only later in chapter 28 will we learn that Aaron and his sons were designated as priests (v24). But early on, God is expressing his vision for his people that they would be a kingdom who would be agents to minister and bring others to him (since that is what priests do).

By this time all nations and city states already had their priests to intercede to their gods. But no nation would have been interested in having a whole kingdom of priests. Who wants an army full of chaplains?

As the priesthood idea is progressively revealed to Israel, we find that God's words to Moses develop more meaning. The priests are called to live a different life, not attaching themselves to the ways of this world:

- They were not to fight, indicated because they were not to be included in the census of those who would be in the army. While fighting was the way people solved most issues in the ancient world, the priests were not allowed by God to participate in war.

  > These are those who were enrolled, whom Moses and Aaron enrolled with the help of the leaders of Israel, twelve men, each representing his ancestral house. So the whole number of the Israelites, by their ancestral houses, from twenty years old and upward, everyone able to go to war in Israel—their whole number was six hundred three thousand five hundred fifty. The Levites, however, were not numbered by their ancestral tribe along with them. The Lord had said to Moses: Only the tribe of Levi you shall not enroll, and you shall not take a census of them with the other Israelites. Rather you shall appoint the Levites over the tabernacle of the covenant, and over all its equipment, and over all that belongs to it; they are to carry the tabernacle and all its equipment, and they shall tend it, and shall camp around the tabernacle. (Numbers 1:44–50 NRSV)

  The census was to determine the number of men available to engage in war, but the priests were not to be counted. They would have a different role.

This distinction was not uncommon; even among pagan nations, priests were often prohibited from engaging in the acts of war.

- They were not to be the owners of any land.

> The priests, who are Levites—indeed the whole tribe of Levi—are to have no allotment or inheritance with Israel. They shall live on the offerings made to the Lord by fire, for that is their inheritance. They shall have no inheritance among their brothers; the Lord is their inheritance, as he promised them. (Deuteronomy 18:1–2)

> They were to put their trust not in land or possessions, but in the Lord. In a special way they were to find all their security in the Lord God.

Just how significant these requirements will be for understanding the kingdom life for a new-covenant people will be evaluated in light of what we will find in the New Testament. But, for now, these references may be giving us some clues as to the tenor of the Kingdom.

We do see this idea of a kingdom of priests again in the Old Testament. It occurs the next time in Isaiah 61, and we will include a lengthy text which brings many key ideas together.

> The Spirit of the Sovereign Lord is on me,
>   because the Lord has anointed me
>   to preach good news to the poor.
> He has sent me to bind up the brokenhearted,

to proclaim freedom for the captives
and release from darkness for the prisoners,
to proclaim the year of the LORD's favor
and the day of vengeance of our God,
to comfort all who mourn,
and provide for those who grieve in Zion—
to bestow on them a crown of beauty
instead of ashes,
the oil of gladness
instead of mourning,
and a garment of praise
instead of a spirit of despair.
They will be called oaks of righteousness,
a planting of the LORD
for the display of his splendor.

They will rebuild the ancient ruins
and restore the places long devastated;
they will renew the ruined cities
that have been devastated for generations.
Aliens will shepherd your flocks;
foreigners will work your fields and vineyards.
And you will be called priests of the LORD,
you will be named ministers of our God.
You will feed on the wealth of nations,
and in their riches you will boast. (Isaiah 61:1–6,
emphasis added)

Later Jesus will clearly identify this as a messianic text
and one he fulfilled as he went out preaching the good news
of the Kingdom (Luke 4:16–21). Those who are in God's
new realm in the day of good news, the year of the Lord's
favor, will be "oaks of righteousness" and will be called

"priests of the Lord." There is no reference to the Kingdom in here but, in light of Jesus' use of the words, this is clearly in a kingdom context, and those people in God's Kingdom will all be serving as priests. As Isaiah concludes his book, there is an astonishing text that seems to predict that even from among the Gentiles, there will be those called to be priests in this new Kingdom (Isaiah 66:18–21).

All of this, of course, is fulfilled in Jesus and the church. After Jesus, Peter will reinforce this point, using Old Testament language to describe kingdom citizens as "a chosen people, a royal priesthood [that is a priesthood of the king], a holy nation" (1 Peter 2:9).

And so as we begin to look for the kingdom concept in the Old Testament, we find that maybe the very clearest thing said is that God wants a nation—a people—who will live in some fashion as priests.

The Jewish State and the Kingdom of God

From the time of the Exodus for four hundred or so years, Israel was a collection of tribes without a monarch. Failing to be secure in their relationship with God as their sovereign and most likely fearing they were at a disadvantage and vulnerable to attack, the people demanded a king (1 Samuel 8:4–5). God granted their wish. After the disastrous reign of the troubled and imbalanced Saul, David ruled Israel in a way that some would, no doubt, believe *was* a realization of the Kingdom of God. He won victory after victory, dramatically expanding Israel's territory and setting up his capital in Jerusalem. He ushered in a time, described gloriously in 2 Samuel 7, that the Jews would look back on fondly and nostalgically for hundreds of years. The Star of David is the symbol of modern Israel in our own day.

David, at one point in his life was described as the man after God's own heart, and Jews and Christians still cherish his psalms. However, with his equally well-known dark side, his was just another human government dogged by scandal. David's Jewish state was his kingdom, not the fulfillment of the Kingdom of God.

His son Solomon took the nation to new heights and built a glorious temple for the worship of God, but personally went to new lows. Following his death, because of his unfaithfulness, his kingdom was rent in two, beginning a national plunge that would involve more than a thousand years of almost uninterrupted humiliating domination by foreign powers. The Jews' cries for an earthly king and a stronger nation state brought some fleeting glory, then a sequence of disasters, but nothing resembling the Kingdom of God.

The prophets who came after Solomon were primarily those who spoke God's word to the current situation, continuing to advocate for the heart attitude that God wanted, calling Israel to repentance. But God also used the prophets to look far down the line to the coming of his Kingdom and to the one who would bring it in. Throughout the writings of the prophets are interwoven various prophecies of what the coming king, the anointed one, the Messiah would be like and what the nature of his Kingdom would be.

John Bright, in his classic work on the Kingdom, points out that in the words of Amos, Hosea, Isaiah and Ezekiel—but particularly in Jeremiah—God made it known that the coming Kingdom would not be linked to the state, although many Jews held tenaciously to that idea. But, in Bright's words,

> Jeremiah's message is a total rejection of the state as a vehicle of the kingdom of God beyond which nothing could be more total.... Whatever covenant had existed between God and the state was broken, finished, and Jeremiah's younger contemporary, Ezekiel, had exactly the same conviction.[4]

God intended to set up a different kind of kingdom that would not be of this world. The prophets give us more clues about the nature of this Kingdom, and we will look at those shortly.

The Messiah and the Kingdom

Before we consider those clues, we must first note that there were two different expectations that were growing in Judaism due to the words of the prophets. First, they began to look for a Messiah (God's anointed) who would bring a new day—a day of deliverance, and second, they looked for the coming of the Kingdom of God—that is Yahweh returning to Zion and demonstrating his rule among men. From our vantage point we easily blend those two ideas together, but it is not clear just how much blending was done by the Jews who were waiting for God to act. It would not be surprising if some merged the two concepts, but judging from Peter's words in 1 Peter 1:10–12, the prophets themselves may not have been able to connect all the dots they were proclaiming through the inspiration of the Spirit. However, as we will see shortly in Isaiah, it does appear that he was one prophet who understood that the two were companion expectations.

Because of Moses' words in Deuteronomy 18:15: "The Lord your God will raise up for you a prophet like me from among your own brothers. You must listen to him"—the Jews had long expected another towering figure who would deliver them. Surely some must have thought for a time that David was that figure, but when history revealed a different conclusion, they looked for another.

David had his kingdom and Solomon had his kingdom. But after this golden age in Israel, various times of chaos, and eventually periods of captivity, the people longed even more for the establishment of God's Kingdom. It is during this time that the prophets came calling for repentance but preaching that God was still at work to bring a new day. They gave more specific reference to the coming Kingdom of God, though they did not use the term, and more clues as to what "the mountain of the Lord" (Isaiah 2:3), "his government and peace" (Isaiah 9:6–7), "my holy mountain" (Isaiah 11:9) would be like. Knowing as we do from the New Testament that the coming of the Messiah is linked with the coming of the new age, we will look at various passages primarily in Isaiah that give us insights into the coming of the king and his Kingdom.

The Prophets and the Kingdom

While clues can be found from other writers, no one gives us more than Isaiah.

He has scarcely begun his book when he gives us the first important kingdom passage. It is found in Isaiah 2:1–6:

> This is what Isaiah son of Amoz saw concerning
>   Judah and Jerusalem:
> In the last days
> the mountain of the LORD's temple will be established
>   as chief among the mountains;
> it will be raised above the hills,
>   and all nations will stream to it.
>
> Many peoples will come and say,
>
> "Come, let us go up to the mountain of the LORD,
>   to the house of the God of Jacob.
> He will teach us his ways,
>   so that we may walk in his paths."
> The law will go out from Zion,
>   the word of the LORD from Jerusalem.
> He will judge between the nations
>   and will settle disputes for many peoples.
> They will beat their swords into plowshares
>   and their spears into pruning hooks.
> Nation will not take up sword against nation,
>   nor will they train for war anymore.

While we cannot say that the image of a mountain in the prophetic writing always refers to kingdoms or that "my holy mountain" always refers to the Kingdom of God, there are a number of places where the context strongly points in this direction. Examples would be this passage and Isaiah 56:6–7, 57:13, 65:21–25, 66:19–21 and Ezekiel 20:39–41. In other passages such as Isaiah 65:11 "my holy mountain" would seem to point more to Mount Zion and the temple, although this too could be related to the Kingdom.

Our present passage, with the phrase "the mountain of the Lord's temple will be established as chief among the mountains," would seem to describe a kingdom from God that is superior to all other kingdoms. Reinforcing this thought is the indication that the scope of "the mountain of the Lord's temple" will go far beyond Israel, affecting nations and many peoples. Also, supporting this thought is the eschatological nature of the passage—that is, it describes what will happen in "the last days." It looks forward to the end times, something clearly associated with the Kingdom of God.

Isaiah describes how the word goes out from Zion (from Jerusalem). It would have been no surprise to the Jews that God intended to launch this new age from the city of David. What would have been surprising, and something the Jews were prone to overlook, is that all nations would be streaming to it. It would not be limited to those who saw themselves as the "chosen." Many peoples (translation: many who were not Jews) would be saying "let's go walk in those paths."

But then we see just how transformational this coming Kingdom would be. It will be a kingdom of peace. It will not just be the Jews who learn to get along with each other (though that in itself would have been transformational), but these nations and these peoples will have their disputes *settled by God*, and "they will beat their swords into plowshares and their spears into pruning hooks. Nation will not take up sword against nation, nor will they train for war anymore." As we will see, this concept of peace among those who once were enemies will be repeated several times in Isaiah, so much so, that we must conclude that a dominant characteristic of those in the Kingdom is that they do not train for war and they do not harm others. They will take their destructive instruments of war, and as a demonstration of kingdom transformation, reshape them into helpful farming instruments. What was once used to destroy life will be used to nourish life. While many Jews pictured the Kingdom being ushered in by those adept at war and those who could defeat the "nations" and the "many peoples," Isaiah has a different vision. In the Kingdom something so dramatic is going to change that this "us" against "them" mentality is going to end.

In Isaiah 7:14 we have the much discussed passage in which the prophet tells us that a young woman ("virgin" in many versions and in the Septuagint, the Greek translation of the Old Testament) will give birth to a child. The text most certainly had a contemporary application, but then in chapter 9 Isaiah seems to develop the idea theologically so that it has more far-reaching meaning. In 9:6–7 he writes of a child (apparently the same one) who is extraordinary and who will rule an exceptional Kingdom:

> For to us a child is born,
>   to us a son is given,
>   and the government will be on his shoulders.
> And he will be called
>   Wonderful Counselor, Mighty God,
>   Everlasting Father, Prince of Peace.
> Of the increase of his government and peace
>   there will be no end.

He will reign on David's throne
　　and over his kingdom,
establishing and upholding it
　　with justice and righteousness
　　from that time on and forever.
The zeal of the LORD Almighty
　　will accomplish this.

This is a most important text from which we draw several key points:

1. We have here the clearest statement that a new Kingdom is coming and the clearest statement that the ideas of the Messiah and the Kingdom should be brought together. The one coming will reign on David's throne and over his kingdom.

2. A government is being described here. It is on the shoulders of the son who is given to us.

3. But this government and Kingdom will not be temporal. To put it another way, after many broken promises of men, we will finally have something that "is not politics as usual." It is a new kind of politics, led by a new kind of leader. And unlike all the governments before it, it will have an everlasting nature—it will be "from that time on and forever."

4. The one who rules in this Kingdom is unlike anyone ever known before. He comes as a child and will be called by several names, including some that ordinarily would be blasphemous: "Wonderful Counselor," which is acceptable, but then "Mighty God" and "Everlasting Father"?

- "Wonderful Counselor" would seem to refer to both the wisdom he will possess and the considerate and gentle way that he will dispense it.
- "Mighty God" (*El Gabor* in Hebrew) appears only two times in the Old Testament as a name: here and in Isaiah 10:21. Clearly in the latter, it refers to God.
- "Everlasting Father" (*Ab-Ad* in Hebrew) is used only here in the Old Testament. Though this raises some issues in Trinitarian thinking, it points to the fact that the child will have a oneness with the Father.
- "Prince of Peace" (*Sar Shalom* in Hebrew) certainly fits with the earlier text in Isaiah 2. In contrast with the military victor the Jews were looking for at the time of Jesus, the Messiah will come as a man of peace, not only bringing peace but bringing it in ways consistent with a character of peace.
- Then finally, his kingly rule will be upheld with justice and righteousness. This Kingdom will not be about suppression, domination and control. It will be about character, care and fair treatment of others.

Two chapters later, Isaiah gives us more insight into the one who is coming, and these thoughts fit well with what we have already seen:

> A shoot will come up from the stump of Jesse;
>   from his roots a Branch will bear fruit.
> The Spirit of the Lord will rest on him—
>   the Spirit of wisdom and of understanding,

the Spirit of counsel and of power,
the Spirit of knowledge and of the fear of the
LORD—
and he will delight in the fear of the LORD.

He will not judge by what he sees with his eyes,
or decide by what he hears with his ears;
but with righteousness he will judge the needy,
with justice he will give decisions for the poor
of the earth.
He will strike the earth with the rod of his mouth;
with the breath of his lips he will slay the
wicked.
Righteousness will be his belt
and faithfulness the sash around his waist.

The wolf will live with the lamb,
the leopard will lie down with the goat,
the calf and the lion and the yearling together;
and a little child will lead them.
The cow will feed with the bear,
their young will lie down together,
and the lion will eat straw like the ox. (Isaiah 11:1–7)

In contrast to what God will do to the foreign invaders in his role as judge—cut them down as a forest thicket is cut down by an ax (10:34)—he will bring forth from a stump and root of Jesse (David's line) a branch that will bear fruit because on him the Spirit will rest in powerful ways.

Think about it. A shoot from a stump: How impressive is that? But this is consistent with Isaiah's vision. The one who is coming and bringing the Kingdom is going to do it according to God's wisdom, not man's. His method will seem unimpressive. There will be nothing showy about it. Peter in Matthew 16 was just one in a long line of people who did not think someone who was lowly in manner could fulfill God's purpose.

That this branch is the Messiah who will rule in righteousness (vv4–5) there is little doubt. And again we see he is bringing a reign where peace among natural enemies will be found. With the little child leading them (as in chapter 9), the wolf will live with the lamb and the calf with the lion, and then come some of the most beautiful words in the Old Testament: "They will neither harm nor destroy on all my holy mountain." Significantly, Isaiah repeats this same line in chapter 65 when he describes the ultimate fulfillment of the Kingdom of God in *the new heavens and the new earth* (vv17–25).

While we cannot speculate on whether there will be animals in heaven (one of us has a wife who surely hopes so), it seems obvious that the animals described here represent kingdom citizens who want nothing but good for others, though they once would have been natural enemies. Can we miss the point that those who once would have killed each other, will do so no longer and will live together in peace?

We should take note that four times now when the Kingdom is described, we have seen that it is a realm where its inhabitants make no war and do no harm and where its leader is described as the Prince of Peace. We have discussed among ourselves how much this understanding should be emphasized. We do not want to present an inaccurate picture or over-emphasize one quality, but in Isaiah this certainly seems to be the dominant characteristic of the coming Kingdom. Read it carefully and see what your conclusion is.

This peaceable and non-violent aspect was given great emphasis by the second- and third-century Christians, but was sadly lost by the early fourth century during the massive paradigm shift that came with Constantine and his worldly ways of "helping" the Christian cause. It is not by any means the only characteristic of the Kingdom, but it seems to stand as a prominent example of the way the kingdoms of the world and the Kingdom of God are so dramatically different.

In Isaiah 11 we also see the Messiah's concern that the needy and the poor receive help and justice (v4). In chapter 32 where we find "a king will reign in righteousness," we again find concern for the hungry and the poor (vv6–7). The text in Isaiah 61, which we have mentioned and which Jesus quoted in Nazareth, likewise speaks of good news for the poor (v1). With the laws in the Torah pertaining to the poor (such as Exodus 22:21–24 and Deuteronomy 10:18ff), it would be surprising if we did not find this same emphasis connected with the Kingdom. Authors Shane Claiborne and Chris Haw have rightly said that something cannot be the good news of the Kingdom unless it is good news for the poor.[5]

Having referred to Isaiah 32, we should also note the special emphasis on relationships that will be found in the Kingdom:

> See, a king will reign in righteousness
> and rulers will rule with justice.

> Each man will be like a shelter from the wind
>   and a refuge from the storm,
> like streams of water in the desert
>   and the shadow of a great rock in a thirsty land.
>   (Isaiah 32:1–2)

Since righteousness is all about relationships and how you handle them, we find that the Old Testament points toward relationships that the New Testament will clarify and emphasize (these are often referred to as "one another" relationships). People will not compete with one another but will protect one another. We are writing this chapter on a cold February day, and the pictures on the television show frozen-looking people walking against a thirty-five-mile-an-hour wind in Washington, D.C., where a massive snow storm has stopped almost all traffic. Each of those folks outside could use some refuge from the wind. Isaiah says kingdom people will be that for each other.

Perhaps you have seen the astonishing film *The March of the Penguins* and can remember how the emperor penguins crowd in with one another in the -55 degree Fahrenheit temperature on the Antarctica plains to provide protection and refuge, and then rotate so that no one has to stay on the outside ring very long. Isaiah sees the king in his righteousness leading his people to treat one another with that kind of mutual concern.

As we survey Isaiah, is it any wonder that many refer to his book as "The Gospel According to Isaiah"? The good news of the Kingdom is found throughout the book.

But we aren't finished. We must still look at Isaiah 42 and 53.

"Here is my servant, whom I uphold,
    my chosen one in whom I delight;
I will put my Spirit on him
    and he will bring justice to the nations.
He will not shout or cry out,
    or raise his voice in the streets.
A bruised reed he will not break,
    and a smoldering wick he will not snuff out.
In faithfulness he will bring forth justice;
    he will not falter or be discouraged
till he establishes justice on earth.
    In his law the islands will put their hope."
    (Isaiah 42:1–4)

We know we are still on the same ground as in the earlier texts, as he speaks of the one who brings justice to the nations. He will not be showy or flamboyant, but unassuming, gentle and compassionate (which fits with the Wonderful Counselor described earlier). Reeds were used for all kinds of purposes, but a bruised reed was usually broken and thrown away. A smoldering wick does more harm than good, creating irritating smoke and little light. But Isaiah beautifully describes one who will not break the bruised reeds or snuff out the smoldering wicks, but who will give them hope and nurse them back to life.

Finally, when we come to Isaiah 53, we reach the holy of holies of the teaching about the Messiah, if not the entire Old Testament. While little or nothing is said here about the Kingdom the way we have found it in other passages, we have already seen enough of a link between the coming Kingdom and the coming "One," that we know we are dealing with the servant who will be living out the kingdom message.

The context actually starts in 52:13, and we find, like earlier, one who affects many nations, has superiority to kings, is like a tender shoot and root out of dry ground, and after his suffering will gain a great victory that will bring deliverance to many (53:11–12). But now we learn that he lives innocently, does no violence, but is pierced for our transgressions and crushed for our iniquities. For the first time, we see the depth of the service and sacrifice of the servant/Messiah/king and learn that the coming of the Kingdom must also involve having our sin healed by his wounds.

Isaiah 53 presents a vision of the coming Messiah that the Jews were not prepared for at that time or even after they had 700 years to contemplate it. When Jesus arrived on the scene, they were expecting, even longing for, a leader armed with worldly power and military prowess who would liberate them from foreign domination. As professor Bright observes, "The Servant [did] not ever catch the popular fancy…. Judaism could not see the Servant as Messiah…. The Jews did not want a suffering Messiah."[6] One who would be despised, smitten, afflicted, pierced, oppressed and crushed would have hardly seemed to qualify for this role of deliverer and liberator. They were slow to learn that God's ways were not their ways (Isaiah 55:8–9).

Perhaps we could summarize the Old Testament vision of the Kingdom like this:

1. Is a kingdom of priests
2. Is for all nations and peoples
3. Will last forever

4. Will be established by God's suffering servant/ Messiah/king
5. Will be committed to the needy and the poor
6. Will be characterized by right relationships inside and out
   - Inside – the citizens will protect and guard each other
   - Outside – they will turn swords into plowshares, learn war no more, reject violence and do no harm

It would not be accurate, of course, to say that the Jewish people understood all this. It certainly was not part of a catechism taught to Jewish children. For it is clear that when John the Baptist and Jesus came, the populace, though looking for the Kingdom, was rife with all sorts of distorted ideas.

The Kingdom: In History or Beyond History?

There was one misunderstanding that the Jewish people had that we cannot blame them for. Indeed, it was one of God's surprises. Jews likely tended to believe one of two things: (1) most believed that the coming of the Kingdom would be so dramatic and decisive that everything on earth would change, with Israel being in complete control, or (2) some may have believed that its coming would be so cataclysmic that history itself would come to an end with the Kingdom being all that was left. There was not a lot of difference in these views. In either case, the Jewish expectation was that Yahweh would judge the nations and vindicate "his people."

A passage like this one in Daniel would seem to have supported either of those conclusions:

> "In the time of those kings [the last of four kingdoms Daniel has already spoken of], the God of heaven will set up a kingdom that will never be destroyed, nor will it be left to another people. It will crush all those kingdoms and bring them to an end, but it will itself endure forever. This is the meaning of the vision of the rock cut out of a mountain, but not by human hands—a rock that broke the iron, the bronze, the clay, the silver and the gold to pieces.
>
> "The great God has shown the king what will take place in the future. The dream is true and the interpretation is trustworthy." (Daniel 2:44–45)

To diagram it, we might say they saw the coming age as beginning like this (see figure 1).

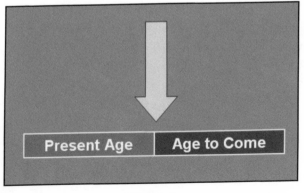

Figure 1

God was coming, judging the nations, bringing an end to this present age and ushering in the age to come. He, through his anointed ruler, the Messiah, would begin a new and glorious age where Jerusalem would be the center of the universe and all would be well in Zion. If the Gentiles, those of the nations, existed at all, they would be completely dominated by the chosen people. Not surprisingly, the Jews overlooked those words indicating God's desire to have those from all nations included in his blessed and forever people.

However, there is another way the words of Daniel 2 (and Daniel 7, the parallel passage that describes again the four earthly kingdoms) could have been read. Clearly God's Kingdom was going to be "set up" during the days of "those kings" (an apparent reference to the Roman Empire), but it may exist for a time in the midst of the earthly kingdoms. It will appear as a rock, small in size in comparison to a mountain. It other words, it may not look like much in comparison to existing kingdoms. But it will eventually crush the other kingdoms, and it will endure forever. While most of us would likely have read Daniel's words the way the Jews did, expecting all he describes to follow in quick succession, Daniel does not tell us what God's timing will be. He just says it will happen. It could happen suddenly or it could happen gradually and eventually. In Jesus and his message the truth will become clear.

When we turn to Jesus in our next chapter, we will see that he spoke early and often about the Kingdom, but not in the ways the Jews expected, and truth be told, not in ways many of us would have expected. As we prepare for the next step in this investigation, we must all pray for open hearts and open minds. A challenge is coming our way.

Questions for Study and Discussion

1. What are some of the different ways that you can see Jesus fulfilling the Law and the Prophets? How do you think what he taught and did went beyond just fulfilling historical details predicted by a prophet?

2. Do you have a positive, negative or neutral view of the role of priest? Why?

3. What do you believe God's plan was when he spoke of wanting his people to be "a kingdom of priests"?

4. If all we had was the message of Isaiah and from that message we sought to live God's will on the earth, what kind of community would we become? What would be distinctive about such a community?

5. How does this compare to what you already know of the life the Christian community is called to in the New Testament?

6. Of the concepts we have looked at, which one brings to you the most conviction and causes you to want to reexamine your own life?

NOTE: We include discussion questions at the end of each chapter, but they are also available on the web with permission to print and copy. (kingdombooks-vol1.blogspot.com)

2
The Kingdom Is Here

JESUS AND THE GOSPEL OF THE KINGDOM

Part One

Having surveyed certain kingdom principles from the Old Testament, we should also remember that for most of the thousand years before Jesus, the Jews had been under the domination of some foreign power—the Assyrians, the Babylonians, the Persians, Alexander the Great, and then his successors, and now at the time of Jesus, the Romans. From our perspective this was God's discipline for their rebelliousness, but it most likely did not seem that way to them.

Both of us have lived in Boston and with all due respect to the New England Patriots (and their three Super Bowl wins in five years), Boston is a baseball town. Between 1918 and 2004—eighty-six years—the team went without winning a World Series. As they saw it, for eighty-six years the citizens of Boston and most of New England were under the domination of a foreign power, primarily the New York Yankees—aka "The Evil Empire." (Certainly New York readers who cheer for the team in the Bronx will see it all differently.)

Every spring Red Sox fans looked forward to opening day in hopes that this would be *the* season when the hated "curse of the Bambino" would be reversed. We were amazed to see that one of the biggest days in Boston every year was that day in February when the equipment truck left Fenway Park headed for Florida because that meant pitchers and catchers were about to report and spring training was about to begin. News teams with their cameras would head for Landsdowne Street to take pictures of a semi driving out of Boston in the direction of Florida. Certain people and mascots would be appointed to escort the truck through the streets to the expressway. Such pictures stirred the passions and aroused the anticipation. By opening day that anticipation would become so thick you could cut it with a knife.

How could this have anything to do with the Kingdom of God and the Jews who waited for it? Like Red Sox fans, the Jewish people were tired of losing, and they longed for deliverance. Every year they thought "Maybe this will be the year when God comes in his Kingdom and vindicates his people and breaks the yoke of this foreign domination and puts the Gentiles in their place." They had read the prophets we talked about in the last chapter, and though they seemed to miss so much of the message, they clung to the idea that there would be a day of the Lord when God would come in his Kingdom. They yearned for it.

And so when John comes saying "the kingdom is near" and Jesus comes saying "the kingdom is in your midst" and "the kingdom has come upon you," this was something that caused a stir in a highly charged situation that was ripe with anticipation.

While the phrase "the Kingdom of God" was not actually found in the Old Testament, we are struck with just how often that phrase is on the lips of Jesus. Let's take note of a few passages that show that the preaching of the Kingdom was at the heart of Jesus' mission.

> **Matthew 4:23** — Jesus went throughout Galilee, teaching in their synagogues, preaching the good news of the kingdom, and healing every disease and sickness among the people.

> **Matthew 9:35** — Jesus went through all the towns and villages, teaching in their synagogues, preaching the good news of the kingdom and healing every disease and sickness.

> **Matthew 24:14** — "And this gospel of the kingdom will be preached in the whole world as a testimony to all nations, and then the end will come."

> **Mark 1:15** — "The time has come," he said. "The kingdom of God is near. Repent and believe the good news!"

> **Luke 4:43** — But he said, "I must preach the good news of the kingdom of God to the other towns also, because that is why I was sent."

Luke 8:1 — After this, Jesus traveled about from one town and village to another, proclaiming the good news of the kingdom of God. The Twelve were with him.

We need to remember from our last chapter how the Jews most likely heard these words. We used the diagram (see figure 1 on page 34) which showed that they expected the coming of the Kingdom to be the end of the present age and the beginning of the age to come. They thought it would be a time when the Jews would rule the other nations, and the Gentiles would either be destroyed or totally dominated, and it would be forever.

But as we get into the message of Jesus, we see that God's plan involved a surprising twist.

What Is This Kingdom?

We have seen that the Jews expected the Kingdom but had different ways of thinking about what it would mean. What exactly did Jesus mean when he talked about the Kingdom? How do you sum it up? Since this concept was so central to his message, we may find it surprising that Jesus never gave us a definition. He did not string together a series of Old Testament texts to show that the Kingdom was fulfilled in any one way or in any one event. Instead to help us understand it, Jesus told stories. Yes, stories and parables that gave us mental pictures. He would say, "The kingdom of heaven/God is like…" and then give us one of the stories or pictures or metaphors. Look at some examples in the Gospel of Matthew.

The Kingdom of God is like

1. A man who sowed good seed in a field (13:24)
2. A mustard seed which a man planted in a field (13:31)
3. Yeast that a woman took and mixed into a large amount of flour (13:33)
4. Treasure hidden in a field (13:44)
5. A merchant looking for pearls (13:45)
6. A net let down in the lake (13:47)
7. A king who wanted to settle accounts with his servants (18:23)
8. Landowner who went early in the morning to hire men to work (20:1)
9. A king who prepared a wedding banquet for his son (22:2)

The very fact that Jesus employed this method to communicate the Kingdom probably tells us a great deal about the Kingdom: It is an expansive, rich and dynamic concept that cannot be boxed or bottled up in nice little formulas, even if that frustrates those who want everything neatly spelled out in black and white.

Have you ever driven around a great mountain and looked at it from different angles? From the east in the morning it looks different than from the west in the evening. From the south at sunset it looks different than from the north at sunrise. No one picture captures it. Surveyors could measure it, geologists could analyze it, botanists could classify its plant life, but you really wouldn't begin to capture the mountain until you brought in the poets, the artists and the songwriters. And there would always be more to learn. In the parables Jesus is doing and saying something like this with the Kingdom. No one phrase or idea completely defines it. You can observe many of its aspects. But beware of anyone who has it all figured out. Get humble if you ever think you have.

Kingdom Characteristics

However, this does not mean that the Kingdom of God in Jesus' teaching was some esoteric concept that you can connect with only in some mystical sort of way. No, while the Kingdom is too great for us to get our arms completely around, there are vital truths we can certainly know and understand about it. We will note several of these.

1. A reign that is now and not yet.

The word for Kingdom, *basileia*, means "reign" or "rule." By definition the Kingdom is all about being under the reign of God. The Kingdom is God in his "Kingness" leading, guiding, directing his people with them submitting to his rule.

In Jesus' teaching, the Kingdom was seen as being in the *now*, but was also viewed as something that was *not yet* here in all its finality. The scholars have called it the "now/ not yet paradox." The Kingdom comes in the now, but the present age (and its fallen nature) doesn't immediately pass away. While one lives the kingdom life now, one also looks forward in hope to that which is not yet. One passage where we see this clearly is Mark 10:29–31.

> "I tell you the truth," Jesus replied, "no one who has left home or brothers or sisters or mother or father or children or fields for *me and the gospel* will fail to receive a hundred times as much in this *present age* (homes, brothers, sisters, mothers, children and fields—and with them, persecutions) and in the *age to come*, eternal life." (emphasis added)

First, note that Jesus links himself to the gospel: "for me and the gospel." It is our contention that Jesus was the embodiment of the Kingdom (Luke 4:21). He lived it. He demonstrated it. It was breaking into the present age in his person. What gospel was he preaching? It was the gospel of the Kingdom. "For me and the gospel"—Jesus and the gospel of the Kingdom are inseparable.

Our main focus here, however, is that *in this present age* disciples will live the gospel of the Kingdom, put everything under God's reign and on his altar, giving up homes, brothers, sisters, mothers, children and fields. But *in this present age* they will receive a hundred fold. In this present age they will receive the blessings of the Kingdom. To use the words of the writer of Hebrews, they will "taste the powers of the coming age" (Hebrews 6:5). But as they experience the future of God breaking into the present, there will be persecutions, which are a stark reminder that disciples are still in the present age where most of the world still lives by its principles and have no desire to conduct their lives by the principles of the age to come.

With Jesus' surprise, there is still *the age to come* in the older sense, when he comes a second time to bring everything to completion and to usher in the new heavens and the new earth (Isaiah 65:17, 66:22; 2 Peter 3:13). Again remember the typical Jewish view before Jesus was what we saw earlier in figure 1.

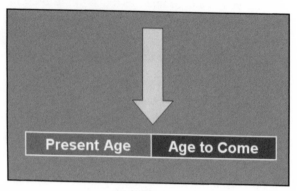

Figure 1

But now we see something quite unexpected—something we might call "the messianic surprise."[1] The age to come is breaking into the present age without fully eliminating it, so that what Jesus teaches about the Kingdom looks more like this (see figure 2).[2]

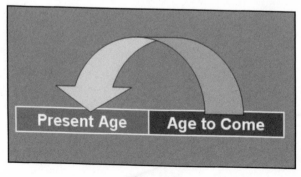

Figure 2

In the coming of the Kingdom, the future has broken into the present age. In God's "kingdom people" you see the new life being lived out in the midst of the old. Everything is not yet set right. However, the Kingdom is a present reality showing up by the power of the Spirit in Jesus and those who follow him. At the same time there is still the promise that the final age to come will one day arrive when everything will be consummated and all will be made right.

A more detailed diagram like the one below (figure 3) shows that the new age and the present age exist simultaneously, as the new age breaks into the present age with the coming of Jesus. This shows that the present age does not end immediately but that those who accept Jesus and receive the Kingdom are living by the new age in the midst of the present age. There will be an eventual end of history when only the new age and its citizens will continue. That end will come at the second coming of Jesus.

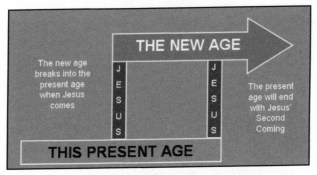

Figure 3

Our friend Douglas Jacoby uses a good illustration (at least for Western audiences) to help us understand the now/not yet paradox. He asks his audience: How many of you own your home? At first many hands go up, but then they sense where this is going. Yes, they own their home now. They can add on to it if they want. They can put shag carpet in it or paint it orange. They also get to fix the plumbing or the heating if needed. They pay taxes on it. They own it now. But do they own it? Not yet, in most cases. There is that little matter of a mortgage. They own it now, but also, not yet.

We have the Kingdom now, but we also do not have it yet. But which should we focus on? The answer is both. We don't just wait for something. We don't just sing, "This world is not my home" and simply sit and think about "treasures somewhere beyond the blue." We go ahead and live the Kingdom now. At the same time, as we live out the Kingdom, and experience the suffering that comes with living it in this present age, the anticipation of a glorious consummation in the future encourages us to persevere. We focus on both the *now* and the *not yet*.[3]

This all leads to a very important conclusion: While the religious world talks a great deal about getting saved so you can go to heaven when you die, *disciples of Jesus will talk more about submitting to Christ so we can start living heaven's way now before we die.* As we do that, we can take great hope and comfort in the truth that a final and complete realization of the Kingdom is coming.

2. An invasion that comes in waves.

The two of us come from a tradition that insisted that the Kingdom came when the church began on Pentecost, and that the Kingdom on earth was essentially the church. This teaching claimed that all references to the Kingdom before Acts 2 implied it had not yet come and all references after Acts 2 implied that it had come. Thus we were able to tell you the day and almost the hour when the Kingdom came. We were even taught not to pray "Your kingdom come," because the Kingdom had already come.

To buttress this idea, reference was made to the fact that both John the Baptist and Jesus said "Repent for the kingdom is near." The implication was that while it was "near," it had not yet arrived. A quick look at some of the ways the word "near" is used in Scripture reveals a quite different understanding.

The writer of Psalm 73 says: "But as for me, it is good to be near God. I have made the Sovereign Lord my refuge; I will tell of all your deeds" (v28). The Hebrew parallelism here means that to be near God is to make him your refuge. In Psalm 34 David writes, "The Lord is near to the broken-hearted and saves those crushed in spirit" (v18, NASB). Again the parallelism means that God being near is equated with his saving action. Isaiah writes, "They ask me for just decisions and seem eager for God to come near them" (58:2). In all of these passages "near" carries the idea that God is *with* them—not "on his way but not here yet." Perhaps the most clarifying text is in Deuteronomy 30:14 where we find, "No, the word is very near you; it is in your mouth and in your heart so you may obey it." It is spelled out for us. Having the word (the command of God) "near you" is to have it be in your mouth, but then even closer, in your heart.

Paul's use of the word "near" is like that of the Old Testament. He writes: "Rejoice in the Lord always. I will say it again: Rejoice! Let your gentleness be evident to all. The Lord is near" (Philippians 4:4–5). The word *eggus*, translated "near" can also be translated, as many older versions do, "at hand" and on occasions translated "ready." It is a form of the same word (*eggizo*) Jesus uses in the Gospels regarding the Kingdom. The context makes it clear that God is an ever-present guard against anxiety and is active in our lives right now. "Near" is in contrast to "far." It is the opposite end of the continuum. As we consider the full complement of Jesus' kingdom teaching, it becomes evident that when he says "the Kingdom is near," he is saying, "the Kingdom is here."

Many of us perk up when someone from the kitchen calls to the family and says, "Dinner is ready." In view of Jesus' parable of the Kingdom in Matthew 22 that says the Kingdom is like a great meal where the host calls out, "Everything is ready, come to the...banquet" (v4), it is easy to hear Jesus saying, "Change your minds and come to the feast. The Kingdom is ready. You don't want it to get cold!"

The idea that the Kingdom came first on Pentecost is flawed. There is an abundance of evidence that the Kingdom was in the process of coming in the life and ministry of Jesus well before Pentecost. We will look at several verses that make this clear, but in appendix 1 you can see these and other passages that show that the Kingdom cannot be made equal to the church. But we use the word "process" because it has occurred to us that as you read the New Testament, you get the sense that the Kingdom does not come in any one moment or even on any one day, but that it is coming in waves.

The award-winning movie *Saving Private Ryan* features a graphic depiction of a famous military invasion. But when did the Allied Forces, depicted in the film, invade France in World War II? The code name for the invasion was Operation Neptune. It officially began on 6 June 1944 (known thereafter as D-Day) at 0630 British time, but then it continued to come in waves all day long. More than that, it actually continued to come in waves for twenty-four more days before it officially ended.

The more we study and consider biblical teaching, the more we think of the Kingdom similarly—as that which was coming in waves.[4]

The Kingdom was clearly coming in Luke 11:19–20:

> "Now if I drive out demons by Beelzebub, by whom do your followers drive them out? So then, they will be your judges. But if I drive out demons by the finger of God, then the kingdom of God has come to you." (NASB—has "come upon you")

When Jesus overthrew the demonic forces, he saw this as an indication that the Kingdom of God was breaking in upon his listeners.

The Kingdom was also coming in Luke 17:20–21:

> Now having been questioned by the Pharisees as to when the kingdom of God was coming, He answered them and said, "The kingdom of God is not coming with signs to be observed; nor will they say,

> 'Look, here it is!' or, 'There it is!' For behold, the
> kingdom of God is in your midst." (NASB)

To those speculating about the Kingdom's arrival, Jesus is saying in so many words, "Open your eyes; the Kingdom is breaking in right in front of you—right under your noses—in me!" This rendering, "in your midst," is just as possible from the Greek and much preferred in this context over the NIV translation—"the kingdom of God is within you,"—since Jesus was certainly not seeing the Kingdom within these hardened Pharisees.

In citing these two verses we do not mean to limit the inbreaking of the Kingdom to these incidents. They are simply evidence that it was coming in Jesus' life—day after day, wave after wave. He very likely made many more statements of this nature (see John 21:25). Jesus himself even taught that the Kingdom began to break in during the ministry of his forerunner. We have these words from Matthew 11:12: "From the days of John the Baptist until now, the Kingdom of heaven has been forcefully advancing, and forceful men lay hold of it."

- When Jesus went into the synagogue in Nazareth, read the prophecy of the Kingdom from Isaiah 61 and said "today this is fulfilled in your hearing," the Kingdom was breaking in.
- When he went up on the mountainside and delivered the Sermon on the Mount or stood on the level place and delivered the Sermon on the Plain, the Kingdom was breaking in (seen in his "You have heard it said…but I tell you" statements).

- When he forgave the paralytic his sins and then told him to rise and walk, the Kingdom was breaking in.

When we view the Kingdom's coming in this way, it causes us to take a fresh look at Mark 9:1:

> And Jesus was saying to them, "Truly I say to you, there are some of those who are standing here who shall not taste death until they see the kingdom of God after it has come with power." (NASB)

If we put aside a preconceived idea that this referred to Pentecost, we may be able to see that it refers to something far more powerful than the events of Pentecost, and we speak here of Jesus' death, burial and resurrection. Is there possibly any place we see the power of Isaiah's suffering servant—the Kingdom's Messiah—coming in a greater way than in Jesus' death and resurrection? Since the age to come will be characterized by self-giving love, have we ever seen a more powerful in-breaking of it than what we see at the cross? John Howard Yoder says it so well:

> Here at the cross is the man who loves his enemies, the man whose righteousness is greater than that of the Pharisees, who being rich became poor, who gives his robe to those who took his cloak, who prays for those who despitefully use him. The cross is not a detour or hurdle on the way to the kingdom, nor is it even the way to the kingdom; it is the kingdom come.[5]

Heaven's wisdom teaches that the one who loses his life, finds it. Do we not see that message powerfully proclaimed as Jesus burst forth from the tomb on Sunday morning? Was this not the monster kingdom wave—the *tsunami?* Did not the future age break powerfully into the present age in the resurrected Jesus, whose body was not a resuscitated corpse but a whole new order of life—showing us something about our own resurrected bodies in the age to come (John 20:26)? And didn't the resurrection of Jesus vindicate his decision to go the way of the cross and show that the cross itself, as the act of self-giving love, was itself a kingdom thing? Again the words of Yoder: "…in the light of the resurrection, crucified agape [selfless love] is not folly (as it seems to the Hellenizers [Greeks]) and weakness (as the Judaizers believe), but the wisdom and power of God (1 Corinthians 1:22–25).[6]

What were the most powerful, decisive, life-altering three days in human history? To use Thomas Cahill's phrase, where do we see the most significant of all the "hinges of history"? Surely for Christians this is none other than the three days that involved the death, the burial and the resurrection of Jesus. In these events everything changed. The law was fulfilled and taken out of the way. The new covenant, not written on tablets of stone but on human hearts, was inaugurated. Jesus became sin so that in him we might become the righteousness of God.

Paul said these events summed up what he called the gospel (1 Corinthians 15:1–4). When he preached the death, burial and resurrection, wasn't he preaching the gospel of the Kingdom come? These events, he called the matters of "first importance." When the church described in Acts preached "the good news of the kingdom" (Acts 8:12, 20:25, 28:31) they were not preaching the good news of the church but the good news of the death and resurrection of Jesus.

Was there ever an invasion of heaven into this present age like this one that pulled together all the elements of the long-awaited Kingdom? Did one series of events over a few days ever fulfill so much Scripture at one time? Can we name another time when God came in his rule in more righteous power? Not even the Second Advent will have all these crucial elements we find in the death and resurrection, for here at the cross, the Lion of Judah loved his enemies and became the lamb that was slain (Revelation 5:5–6). Then "through the Spirit of holiness [he] was declared with power to be the Son of God by his resurrection from the dead…" (Romans 1:4).

It was these events that made Pentecost possible. Indeed it is these events that make everything possible for Christians. It is these events that will infuse every baptism by a repentant person with power until the end of the age. We proclaim these truths, not just to support a point, but to express a sense of awe in regard to God's powerful work at the cross and in the resurrection.[7]

But this is not the end of the story. The Spirit *was* unleashed *on Pentecost*, and the gospel of the Kingdom was preached after the resurrection. Thousands responded in repentance and baptism, and the Kingdom just kept breaking in, first in Jerusalem, then Samaria and then in more places and on to the ends of the earth. Should we doubt that more waves can come? Shouldn't we be praying each day for new waves?

3. A gift to be received.

Jesus' message is the gospel—the good news—of the Kingdom. It is the good news of what God is doing for his people. It is something he is giving, which is to say that it is an act of his grace. It is something he is pleased to offer us as Jesus makes clear in Luke 12:32: "Do not be afraid, little flock, for your Father has been pleased to give you the kingdom." In a context of strong and challenging kingdom teaching (e.g., "don't worry," "sell your possessions," "seek the kingdom"), Jesus tells his disciples not to fear but to understand that the Father is giving them the Kingdom. It is a gift that God offers us, and he gives no gifts that will mock us or harm us, but only gifts that are good (Matthew 7:9–11, Luke 11:11–13.). The Kingdom is his gift.

As John Bright observes, "The people of God are summoned to the side of God's Kingdom in the cosmic struggle, but they cannot produce the Kingdom in terms of their own activity."[8] The Kingdom cannot come through fighting; the Maccabees 150 years before Jesus show us that. It cannot be "lawed" as we see in the Scribes and Pharisees. The Kingdom comes in its own way on God's own time. It is a gift we can only receive with the greatest of humility as we see in Mark 10:13–15:

> People were bringing little children to Jesus to have him touch them, but the disciples rebuked them. When Jesus saw this, he was indignant. He said to them, "Let the little children come to me, and do not hinder them, for the kingdom of God belongs to such as these. I tell you the truth, anyone who will not receive the kingdom of God like a little child will never enter it."

When you think about the keys to the Kingdom, do you think about this passage? No one enters the Kingdom unless they receive the gift like a little child.

In one of the later books of the New Testament, we have the writer of Hebrews giving us a relevant truth:

> Therefore, since we are receiving a kingdom that cannot be shaken, let us be thankful, and so worship God acceptably with reverence and awe....
> (Hebrews 12:28)

It is significant that he does not say we have "received" (past tense) a kingdom. Instead the Greek word is a present active participle which indicates continuing action. We "are receiving" a kingdom.[9] We receive it, and then we receive more of it. We keep on receiving it. One should not think of himself as having received the Kingdom on, for example, February 17, 1998, though that may be the day he confessed "Jesus is Lord" and was baptized in his name. We initially received the Kingdom at our baptism, but we should think of ourselves as those who keep receiving the Kingdom more and more all the time.

As the two of us have devoted ourselves to studying the kingdom message for the last two years, we continue to be challenged to have the heart of a child and receive it in new ways. It is the gift that keeps on giving, as well as the message that keeps calling for our humble response and sincere obedience.

In the next chapter, we will look at more characteristics of the Kingdom that Jesus clearly describes.

Questions for Study and Discussion

1. If Jesus made the good news of the Kingdom his major message, what are some of the implications for us? If we fail to make it a major emphasis in our lives, what will be the effects?

2. What effect does it have on you to understand that the Kingdom of God was fully embodied in Jesus—that to be with Jesus was to see the Kingdom come?

3. What will likely be the outcome if we fail to keep a balance between the "now" and "not yet" nature of the Kingdom?

4. What do you think of the idea of the Kingdom coming in waves in the life of Jesus?

5. Explain why the authors believe the cross and the resurrection should be seen as the supreme moment when the Kingdom came with power? What are your thoughts?

6. What kind of attitudes or actions will bring fresh waves of the Kingdom in our own day?

7. If the Kingdom is *a gift* that we receive, what are some responses that Christians can have that seem to betray this idea?

8. What should be our reaction to being given a great gift?

9. When will someone likely not feel like the Kingdom and its call to action is such a gift?

10. How does receiving the gift of the Kingdom like a child fit with the whole tenor of the kingdom message?

NOTE: We include discussion questions at the end of each chapter, but they are also available on the web with permission to print and copy. (kingdombooks-vol1.blogspot.com)

3

The Kingdom Is Here

JESUS AND THE GOSPEL OF THE KINGDOM

Part Two

In the previous chapter we saw that the kingdom is (1) a reality that is *now* but also *not yet*, (2) the in-breaking of God that comes in waves, and (3) a gift God keeps on giving and one we must keep on receiving. Now we consider more kingdom facts from the teaching of Jesus.

4. A realm to be entered.

The Kingdom is a gift that is offered and is to be received, and receiving the offer brings us into a whole new world. But it is so new and so different that some dramatic changes have to take place for us to enter it.

First, the Kingdom is entered through repentance. Both John the Baptist and Jesus came preaching that everyone must repent to receive the Kingdom (Matthew 3:11, 4:17; Mark 1:4, 15). The word for repentance is *metanoia* (METAN-O-AH) in Greek, which refers to a radical turning. From John to Jesus to Peter to Paul, the message is the same. The Kingdom is so different that we cannot enter it without an immense shift of our thinking.[1]

An Internet search for the country of Molossia will reveal the story of Kevin Baugh, who in 1977 at age fifteen along with a teenage friend, James Spielman, created their own country, just for fun. The Grand Republic of Vuldstein, later renamed the Republic of Molossia, began as they drew a map, created paper money and made a flag. Today Baugh continues his micro-nation with its own website on 1.3 acres in the Nevada desert, still just for the fun of it. He assured a Chicago Tribune reporter that he still pays US taxes, which he calls "foreign aid." "It's always tongue in cheek," Baugh stated. "I'm doing this for the pleasure and enjoyment of having my own country." Through the years, of course, he has always been the chief executive, serving at different times as prime minister, premier and president.

While we may not create our own nation, until we re-pent we are ruling over the kingdom of our own heart, still living by our own plan and flying our own flag. We may send God's Kingdom a little "foreign aid," but it is our kingdom we are seeking first. In repentance, we turn away from our agenda and open ourselves to a whole new way to live. We come with a willingness—no, more than that, an eagerness—to let God define life. We give up our sover-eignty and acknowledge the sovereignty of God.[2]

We can clearly identify two vital elements in the repentance Jesus calls for.

1) Humility—We saw this quality in the earlier passage from Mark 10, but it is even clearer in this one from Matthew 18:

> At that time the disciples came to Jesus and asked, "Who is the greatest in the kingdom of heaven?"
>
> He called a little child and had him stand among them. And he said: "I tell you the truth, unless you change and become like little children, you will never enter the kingdom of heaven. Therefore, whoever humbles himself like this child is the greatest in the kingdom of heaven." (vv1–4)

One of us spoke recently with a group of ten or so Christians who had become disciples as adults. When asked what they had thought about humility before they began to study the Scriptures, they said it was something they had never thought about and had certainly never sought to have.

To get into the Kingdom of God we must experience a radical shift of heart and mind. We have to humble ourselves like little children and admit that we need to listen to our Father, *and* to listen to others who can teach us about our Father.

Jesus calls us to make changes that we will struggle with, but we must ultimately respond with humility. Without humility, no one will enter the Kingdom, or remain in it, for that matter. Again, the word for Kingdom, means "reign" or "rule." To be a kingdom person means being under the reign

of God. This means pride, and self-seeking, and holding
on to our right to our agenda have no place there. Without a turning from pride to humility, we will not enter the
Kingdom.

2) Surrender—Closely related to humility, surrender is at
the heart of placing ourselves under God's reign. And here
we come to arguably the greatest single idea to help us understand what the Kingdom of God is all about. (So if it is
late and you are drowsy either *wake up* or get some sleep
and come back with a clear mind. This is crucial.)

In what is popularly called "The Lord's Prayer," or what
might well be called "The Kingdom Prayer," Jesus teaches
us to pray like this:

> "…your kingdom come;
> Your will be done
> on earth as it is in heaven." (Matthew 6:10)

No one could possibly guess how many times those
words have been mouthed over the past two millennia. In
some traditions they are repeated mindlessly over and over
within the Lord's Prayer to work off some wrongdoing. They
have been repeated by thousands of players before thousands of sporting events and on countless other occasions
where those verbalizing them had no clue as to what they
were saying.

It is really quite astonishing how something so revolutionary could be mangled, mumbled and jumbled into
something so mundane, but then man has always seemed

so adept at practicing a form of godliness but denying its power (2 Timothy 3:5).

But here is the message of this prayer: In the radical step called repentance we turn from seeking our own will to surrendering to God's will, which means seeking *to do* his will. This passage is the key to understanding the ideas we have already considered. In the Greek text you actually have three lines that begin with the phrase "Let your…":

- Let your name be revered.
- Let your kingdom come.
- Let your will be done on earth as it is in heaven.

The last two lines are a classic example of the Hebrew parallelism we find so often in the Psalms. In this poetic device, the second line clarifies or emphasizes the first line. And so *your kingdom come = your will being done on earth as it is in heaven*. The Kingdom of God is the reign of God, and the Kingdom comes to our lives when we give up our will and do his will. The Kingdom is populated by those people who are all saying, "Your will be done."

But, then comes the real revolutionary nature of this prayer. We see here the idea of *the future breaking into the present* because the goal is taking "as it is in heaven" and living it on earth in the here and now. As the future was breaking in with Jesus, so we can let the future break into our present lives.

- Will I be kind in heaven? Yes, so live it now.
- Will I lust in heaven? No, so be done with it here.
- Will I be loving in heaven? Yes, live it now.
- Will I love an enemy in heaven? Yes, so love him now.
- Will I kill in heaven? Of course not, so don't do it here.
- Will I be defensive and self-protective in heaven? No, so banish it now.
- Will I be generous in heaven? Sure, so start practicing it now.
- Do you get the idea?

Once we understand this idea of "living heaven now on earth," so many of the "unreasonable" things Jesus says to do in the Sermon on the Mount begin to make sense. But then we realize that this is not one of several paths we can choose to walk with Jesus. This is the one and only kingdom life. On many computer games you can dial up the level of difficulty you want. We must understand that this is not level ten among nine other levels to choose from. Jesus says this is how we should pray and this is how we should live. However, it is worse than bad to pray these words if we don't mean them.

While we must resist trying to bottle the Kingdom up in a formula, we will never do better than to understand that the Kingdom comes—it breaks in—when we surrender to doing God's will on earth here and now *just as it is in heaven*.

Second, the Kingdom is entered by new birth. A Pharisee with a relatively open heart came to Jesus with nothing but praise for Jesus' ministry and work. He did not bring up the Kingdom of God, but Jesus did. Here is John's account:

Now there was a man of the Pharisees named Nicodemus, a member of the Jewish ruling council. He came to Jesus at night and said, "Rabbi, we know you are a teacher who has come from God. For no one could perform the miraculous signs you are doing if God were not with him."

In reply Jesus declared, "I tell you the truth, no one can see the kingdom of God unless he is born again."

"How can a man be born when he is old?" Nicodemus asked. "Surely he cannot enter a second time into his mother's womb to be born!"

Jesus answered, "I tell you the truth, no one can enter the kingdom of God unless he is born of water and the Spirit." (John 3:1–5)

One can only enter the Kingdom of God through the new birth, or, as it can be translated "the birth from above"—a birth from the age to come. In the first three Gospels we have a horizontal dualism—the present age in contrast with the age to come. In John's Gospel we see Jesus also using a vertical dualism—the world below in contrast with the world above. Both refer to the same dichotomy that can be diagrammed this way (see figure 4).

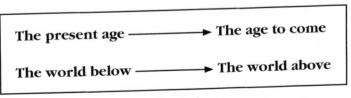

Figure 4

Or from another angle (see figure 5):

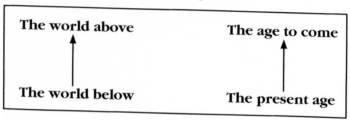

Figure 5

In order to be in the Kingdom, one must experience a birth that comes from the new age.

The Kingdom life is so radically different from normal life in this present age that no one can live it without this act of regeneration. This radical Kingdom calls for a radical response—a putting to death of an old life and the beginning of a new life *empowered by the Spirit.* This is what the apostles taught the crowd in Acts 2 when they called them to repentance and baptism so their sins could be forgiven and so they could receive the gift of the Holy Spirit. The only people who can live the kingdom life are those who are reborn from above and are being transformed by the Holy Spirit.

While many evangelicals today take great pains to disconnect these words in John 3 from baptism and the consequent gift of the Holy Spirit, the overwhelming message of the early church writers (Justin, Ireneus, Tertullian and others) was that this new birth of water and the Spirit referred to what took place in the response of repentance and baptism.[3]

Famed British Baptist scholar G.R. Beasley-Murray, whose classic study *Baptism in the New Testament* will likely never be surpassed on this subject, says that "…in John 3:3–5 [baptism] is the occasion when the Spirit gives to faith the regeneration that qualifies for the Kingdom."[4]

Continuing his thoughts on John 3 Beasley-Murray writes,

> Baptism thus gives hope of resurrection unto the Kingdom by bringing the life of the Kingdom into this one. It is the sacrament of realized eschatology for the inheritance of consummated glory.[5]

Don't be spooked by the scholarly language. He is saying that in baptism the Holy Spirit works to give to our faith the new birth that allows us to be in the Kingdom. And it is the act in which the future age breaks into our lives now, assuring us of the glory that will be ours when the Kingdom comes in its final form. In addition, in baptism we are united with the most powerful of kingdom waves—the death, burial and resurrection of Jesus (Romans 6:1–4).

Repentance and baptism are not hoops for one to jump through to get into the Kingdom. They are not two courses to pass to receive your degree. They are not human works that merit salvation. One cannot enter the Kingdom without repentance and new birth because one cannot do God's will on earth as it is in heaven without turning toward heaven and getting power and new life from above. Repentance is our turning to God. The new birth is God giving to us the essence we need to live in the new world. We cannot enter the Kingdom or live in it without both.

Every time we see a baptism of one who is surrendering to Jesus as Lord, we are seeing the future break in and heaven overlapping with earth. We are seeing one enter the Kingdom.

5. A kingdom totally unlike the kingdoms of this world.

The Kingdom of God will be manifest in this world, but it is not a kingdom *of* this world, meaning it is not a kingdom *like* the kingdoms of this world. In John 18:36 Jesus said, "My kingdom is not of this world. If it were, my servants would fight to prevent my arrest by the Jews. But now my kingdom is from another place."

The kingdoms of this world operate by the world's wisdom. The Kingdom of God operates by God's wisdom. The kingdoms of this world fight and exercise force. Because his Kingdom is not of this world, because it is the Kingdom Isaiah promised where men beat their swords into farming implements, Jesus' disciples will not use violence, nor will they lie or manipulate or cover up as the kingdoms of this world do. The Kingdom does operate *in* this world. But it does not conduct itself *like* the kingdoms of this world. It is engaged in an ongoing war, not against flesh and blood but against the spiritual forces of evil (Ephesians 6:12). In Paul's words:

> For though we live in the world, we do not wage war as the world does. The weapons we fight with are not the weapons of the world. On the contrary, they have divine power to demolish strongholds. We demolish arguments and every pretension that sets itself up against the knowledge of God, and we take captive every thought to make it obedient to Christ. (2 Corinthians 10:3–5)

Since Christians are not armed with the weapons of this world, then with what do they battle against these evil spiritual hosts? Paul's answer was given earlier: "in truthful speech and in the power of God; with weapons of righteousness in the right hand and in the left" (2 Corinthians 6:7). To the Ephesians he listed those weapons: truth, righteousness, the gospel of peace, faith, salvation, the word of God and prayer (Ephesians 6:14–18). The kingdoms of this world might occasionally say a kind word about such things, but they put their confidence someplace else.

Mark it down: Every kingdom of this world operates by the world's wisdom—all 192 or so of them. Some kingdoms or nations/states are more morally repugnant than others, but they all operate by the world's wisdom—your country, our country, all countries. If we have a patriotic zeal that blinds us to this truth, we need to clarify our vision. If you are from France or Russia or Kenya or Iraq or India or Australia or Venezuela or the United States or any of the other countries, your country operates according to the world's wisdom.

Christians in the Kingdom of God understand that they are ultimately, first and foremost, citizens of heaven (Philippians 3:20). As such they can never align themselves with their own physical nation against some other nation. Christians in the various nations comprise a citizenry of heaven that supersedes all other loyalties. For example, American disciples of Jesus have more in common with disciples halfway around the world who live under a dictatorship or a totalitarian regime than we do with our non-disciple neighbor across the street who flies the flag, shoots fireworks on the Fourth of July, wears red, white and blue sneakers, and has a bumper sticker that says "America: Love it or Leave It." If we find we have more affinity with the non-disciple because we share the same national identity, we have missed the gospel of the Kingdom.

As Craig Watts has written, "To the extent that the church willingly shares in the divisions of the world, reflecting them in its own life, it has betrayed the one Lord.... Home for Christians is the church, not the nation."[6] Nationalism is an enemy of the gospel of the Kingdom, just as surely as is racism, classism or sexism.

This is not an anti-American diatribe. The gospel of the Kingdom does not call us to hate our country but to realize that we are "world Christians." I (Steve) lived for eight years in Argentina and have traveled widely in Mexico, Central American and South America. Our job as disciples was never to carry our US brand of government, thoughts and culture to those places, but to relate to them and their culture as we preached the Kingdom. And so, while we are not called to hate our country, we must be careful not to be enamored by it, and we must not unreservedly pledge allegiance to any kingdom except the Kingdom of God.

We believe that Paul's statement in 2 Corinthians 6 has been applied in too narrow a way. Speaking of the distinction between those in the Kingdom of God and those outside it, Paul writes:

> Do not be yoked together with unbelievers. For what do righteousness and wickedness have in common? Or what fellowship can light have with darkness? What harmony is there between Christ and Belial? What does a believer have in common

with an unbeliever? What agreement is there between the temple of God and idols? For we are the
temple of the living God. As God has said: "I will
live with them and walk among them, and I will be
their God, and they will be my people."

"Therefore come out from them
    and be separate, says the Lord.
Touch no unclean thing,
    and I will receive you."
"I will be a Father to you,
    and you will be my sons and daughters,
    says the Lord Almighty." (vv14–18)

Most readers will hear this passage and think of the need
for Christians to only date and marry Christians. We know
of no yoke that is more profound than marriage, and would
wholeheartedly agree with that application. But we must
not let this be our only use of this text. The Old Testament
passages that he quotes have to do with God's people getting involved with other nations. This is where we who are
citizens of heaven need to ask some hard questions about
yoking ourselves with others in the kingdoms of this world in
political, military or governmental processes that operate not
according to God's wisdom but according to man's wisdom.

Evangelical Christians in the US are noted for their involvement in partisan politics, so much so that many people
now equate the whole of US evangelicals with a certain
political party and a certain political ideology. It is this very
yoking together with the kingdoms of this world that we hear
Paul challenging. Such a partnering leads to an acceptance

of worldly means and attitudes, compromises made in the name of expediency, and the alienation—for the wrong reasons—of unbelievers who need to hear the gospel.[7]

Let us look at one example that involves a deep sense of "yoking." From time to time we hear of disciples of Jesus who enlist in the armed services after they become Christians. We wonder if they have thought this through in light of kingdom principles. In enlisting they are yoking themselves with an institution in ways seldom seen in democratic societies. The website *Military.com* encourages military service but gives this word to potential inductees:

> You have to be prepared to drop everything you're doing and leave everything you love in the name of duty. The hours are long, the pay is lousy and the working conditions can be totally brutal and if you stay around long enough, friends die and you will see combat. It is the true nature of military life.

In other words you are yoking yourself with an institution that may send you anywhere in the world anytime it wants to. Whatever it commands you must be ready to do in the name of duty to the nation. When being inducted, each new recruit must take the following oath:

> I, (*NAME*), do solemnly swear (or affirm) that I will support and defend the Constitution of the United States against all enemies, foreign and domestic; that I will bear true faith and allegiance to the same; and that I will obey the orders of the President of the United States and the

orders of the officers appointed over me, according to regulations and the Uniform Code of Military Justice. So help me God.

Enlisting in one of the services involves a rare, and from one perspective, noble form of commitment, most unlike what is asked of other jobs. It involves giving up one's rights out of sense of duty. But it is a commitment, *made in the name of God*, to defend a nation and to obey whatever orders you are given by those above you in the chain of command. It is a commitment to take a certain posture against enemies—a posture very different from the one taught by Jesus (Matthew 5:44). It is not the role of a servicewoman or serviceman to question the ethics of a military operation. It is their role to obey, and they solemnly swear to do that. Tennyson well described the role of the soldier in his famous poem:

> "Forward, the Light Brigade!"
> Was there a man dismay'd?
> Not tho' the soldier knew
> Someone had blunder'd:
> Theirs not to make reply,
> Theirs not to reason why,
> Theirs but to do and die:[8]

It is our conviction that we must seriously evaluate Paul words to not yoke ourselves in deep commitments to unbelievers. The Sermon on the Mount has little, if anything, in common with the codes of this world.

While this may be a fairly obvious application of the kingdom principle, it is by no means the only one that needs to be made. Peter will later remind us that because of our loyalty to heaven, we are aliens and strangers in this world (1 Peter2:11). It is our conviction that if we are truly living as citizens of God's Kingdom, our approach will be so different that we will not be drawn to partnerships with those not committed to God's values.

Early Christians held this conviction about separation from the world for almost three hundred years. They understood that the Kingdom had implications for how they were to be involved in any of this world's kingdoms and how they viewed what we call patriotism. But then came the famous event at the Milvian Bridge, and the yoking together was bid Godspeed by the emperor. As obedient children, we need to wrestle with such issues, seeking the mind of Christ, praying for God's will to be done on earth as it is in heaven.

6. A kingdom bonded to the church, but not the same as the church.

There is a vital overlap between the Kingdom and the church, but there is also a distinction between the two. While many have been taught that the Kingdom is the church, this does not fit with Jesus' teaching and will hinder our understanding of kingdom theology and life. For one thing it often leads to thinking of the Kingdom in institutional terms instead of thinking of it as life and character being shaped by God in his "Kingness"—his rule and his reign.[9]

The Kingdom and the church have the closest possible connection, but the Kingdom and the church are not the very same. No analogy we have found fully captures this relationship, but consider this. The United States Congress comes as close to representing the people of the nation as perhaps any group. All members of Congress are US citizens and they take an oath to support the constitution of the nation. Congressmen and Congresswomen spend most of their time talking about the nation, *but* Congress is not the nation. The nation is greater than Congress. The church in this analogy is more like Congress. Its role is to represent the Kingdom and to speak of the Kingdom, but the Kingdom is something much larger in scope than the church.

This relationship is sometimes described in more complicated ways, but we think we can sum it up with three points.[10]

1. The church is not the Kingdom. The Kingdom is something much larger in scope than the church, and there are dozens of passages in which you just cannot substitute the word "church" for Kingdom (see appendix 1). And by the way, it is especially wrong to think of the Kingdom as any one church group or any one family of churches. To speak of the Kingdom of God in narrow sectarian terms is the height of pride and arrogance. It is most offensive to a majestic idea and truth. It is most disrespectful to the King of the Kingdom. No one group has a corner on the reign of God. It is his and no one else's. "And the Lord knows those that are his" (2 Timothy 2:19).

2. The Kingdom creates the church. As the reign of God breaks into this world in Jesus, it is the Kingdom that creates the church. Jesus as the embodiment of the Kingdom, and Jesus as the resurrection and the life, is the one who calls the church into being. The church owes its life to the Kingdom as we see it in Jesus. The good news of the Kingdom was preached and shown before the church came into being, but at the right time when Jesus returned to the Father, the church was called into service to carry on his work.

So if some of us once explained that all the various texts in Acts 2 fit with the idea that the Kingdom has come, we weren't entirely wrong, even though we used some scripture incorrectly. But we were wrong to teach that the Kingdom started on the day of Pentecost. The Kingdom had been breaking into this age in Jesus, his ministry, his servanthood, his healing, his sacrificial death, his resurrection. Then in Acts 2 on Pentecost the Kingdom is breaking in through the Holy Spirit's power to create the church.

3. The church bears witness to the Kingdom in word and in deed. As the church follows Jesus, and as it functions as the body of Christ, it has as one of its chief roles to preach the good news of the Kingdom just as he did (i.e., see Acts 8:12). The church shares with others the keys to the Kingdom, helps them to enter it, and continues daily to live out the message of the Kingdom.

Philippians 3:20 is again important: "Our citizenship is in heaven." The church is to be a colony of heaven, an outpost of the age to come in the present age. The power of Jesus' message came from the fact that he taught *and* lived it (Acts 1:1). The church must be living the kingdom life, must be distinctive from the world. Otherwise, its message is hollow.

And so what is the Kingdom? The Kingdom is the reign of God. It is where you see God in his "Kingness" ruling and reigning. What is the church? The church is the corporate fellowship, the *koinonia*, of those who have received the Kingdom—the reign of God—and have committed themselves to live out *together* the Kingdom…now…in this world, this present age. As such the church has the highest calling and the deepest union with Jesus. The New Testament uses personal and affectionate language: It is the body of Christ (1 Corinthians 12:27, Ephesians 4:12). It is the Bride of Christ (Ephesians 5:25–32).

So what does it mean to seek first the Kingdom of God? Does it mean to put the church first as some have taught? No, that is too narrow. It means putting first doing and yielding to the will of God on earth as it is in heaven. But will a kingdom-first person be committed to the church? Absolutely, because it is God's family who will show the Kingdom to the world and take the message to the nations.

Let us add one element to the diagram that we used previously to see the place of the church (see figure 6).

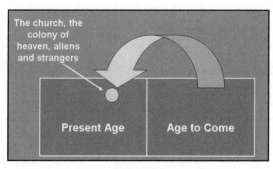

Figure 6

The church is that colony of heaven and of the Kingdom planted squarely in the midst of the world to live as those who have tasted the powers of the age to come (Hebrews 6:5). As such it will announce the Kingdom to the present age. It will be seen as a body of aliens and strangers and will receive opposition from the world around it. It is precisely in this context that the last of the eight Beatitudes rings true: "Blessed are those who are persecuted because of righteousness, for theirs is the kingdom of heaven" (Matthew 5:10).[11]

However, even as it is opposed, the church will bear witness to the truth of Jesus and the Kingdom, and as he says just four verses later in Matthew 5:14, "You are the light of the world. A city on a hill cannot be hidden." The church that is under the reign of God will be a light to the nations.

6. The Kingdom is a life to be lived.

The gospel of the Kingdom does not call us to "get saved so we can go to heaven when we die." That is an almost ubiquitous idea in the evangelical world, but one that is fundamentally selfish. The good news of the Kingdom, instead, calls us to be reborn into a new humanity, and to live out this new humanity in this world now. So instead of talking mostly about how we want to go to heaven when we die, we ought to be focusing on *how to live heaven before we die.* Looking ahead to our final destination in the new heavens and new earth is entirely biblical and right, but only those who want to live out heaven's values *now* are preparing themselves to be heaven's person *then*. In a recent poll 80 percent of Americans said they believe they are going to heaven when they die. But how many of those want to live by heaven's values right now? Not many, said Jesus, warning that there would be some startling surprises come Judgment Day (Matthew 7:21–23).

We will summarize living the kingdom life with three points. Looking at these will bring together much that we have said and bring us around full circle to where we started in the Old Testament.

1. It means living as disciples. It is in the context of kingdom theology that the meaning of discipleship becomes rich and full. Jesus is the Kingdom embodied (see Luke 4:20–21 in context). He calls us to come and follow him, to learn from him, to be his students, to be his disciples. His disciples are those who want to be like him—to interact with family, with friends, with fellow disciples, with strangers and with enemies as he did. He loved them all, cared for them and shared with them the good news. The kingdom life is one of servanthood and cross-bearing. The disciples learned this in an incident recorded in Mark 10:

> When the ten heard about this, they became indignant with James and John. Jesus called them together and said, "You know that those who are regarded as rulers of the Gentiles lord it over them, and their high officials exercise authority over them. Not so with you. Instead, whoever wants to become great among you must be your servant, and whoever

> wants to be first must be slave of all. For even the Son
> of Man did not come to be served, but to serve, and
> to give his life as a ransom for many." (vv41–45)

The kingdoms of the world—the nations/states of our contemporary world—function through the exercise of authority, some surely with a more heavy hand than others. While the exercising of this authority is often fraught with abuses, God, nonetheless, uses it to maintain order in societies (Romans 13). However, those in the Kingdom are not here for that civil purpose, but are here to announce a whole new way of relating to people and to model it for the world. "Not so with you!" Jesus says. This is not the way of the Kingdom. The kingdom way is the way of the servant, the way of those who exercise no dominating power, the way of those who voluntarily lay down their lives for others. Consequently, kingdom leadership will be dramatically different from what is typical in the world. When church leadership is not kingdom-style leadership, great damage is done as many can testify to.

Jesus is the suffering servant that Isaiah spoke of, and the kingdom life is one of wanting to know Christ and the fellowship of sharing in his suffering (Philippians 3:10). As disciples of Jesus, kingdom citizens will live a crucified life described by Paul in this passage from 2 Corinthians: "For we who are alive are always being given over to death for Jesus' sake, so that his life may be revealed in our mortal body" (4:11). We don't just thank God for the cross that saved us; we pray to God that we might share it with Christ.

Peter initially struggled with the whole idea of the cross (see Matthew 16), but he learned and then taught that the way of the Kingdom is the way of the cross: "To this you were called, because Christ suffered for you, leaving you an example, that you should follow in his steps" (1 Peter 2:21). Any idea of being a Christian and not being a disciple who follows Jesus is completely foreign to the New Testament.

2. It means living as citizens of heaven. We have referred to this truth a number of times, but to reiterate it, consider two texts from Philippians 3:

> I want to know Christ and the power of his resurrection and the fellowship of sharing in his sufferings, becoming like him in his death... (v10)

> But our citizenship is in heaven. And we eagerly await a Savior from there, the Lord Jesus Christ.... (v20)

We have probably all heard about the three most important words in real estate: LOCATION, LOCATION, LOCATION. When it comes to biblical interpretation we might say that there are also three most important words: CONTEXT, CONTEXT, CONTEXT. And what is the context of Paul's statement? It is in a letter to the Philippian church, and Philippi was a very proud city (a colony of Rome founded by former military men) that had been so loyal to Rome that it had been granted Roman citizenship, something only a few cities could boast.

In this context a number of things in Paul's letter are quite remarkable. For example, Christ is said to have had equality with God, but he emptied himself and became obedient, "even to death on a cross" (2:9). One of the benefits of Roman citizenship was that you could never be put to death by crucifixion, and yet Jesus willingly went there. And now Paul says, "Have in you the same attitude of Jesus." But more to our point here, Paul's statement about citizenship would have caught their attention in a big way. People in Philippi were proud of their Roman citizenship. It had a major impact on their way of life. But Paul points out that they have a higher loyalty that must supersede all other loyalties.

"Our citizenship is in heaven." No doubt they were accustomed to getting their identity from their Roman citizenship, but now they needed to understand that this earthly citizenship paled in comparison to their citizenship in God's Kingdom. While there were certain ways Roman citizens were to conduct themselves and show loyalty to the emperor, the Christians are now called to see how to conduct themselves by looking to heaven and called to be faithful to their king even if this means sharing in the suffering of Christ. Before we are citizens of Russia, Venezuela, Germany, Nigeria, the Philippines or the United States, we are citizens of heaven.

As citizens of heaven, the Sermon on the Mount and the other words of Jesus are our constitution—our manifesto. Our loyalty is to uphold and live his words. As the two of us have taught on the Kingdom in many cities and several countries in the last two years, we have found some Christians who struggle mightily with some of Jesus' words— words we have often ignored. Others who, like the two of us, have been disciples for many years, were ready to obey, but still greatly challenged. Knowing the unpopularity of parts of Jesus' message, we had to search our own hearts and pray for the courage to preach and teach and live what we had learned.

From a worldly point of view, the Sermon on the Mount is a ridiculously hard way to live. In my earlier book on Jesus, I (Tom) shared Philip Yancey's story about students at a major Texas university who found the Sermon to be full of unreasonable ideas, with one saying it was stupid and inhuman.[12] We suspect many Americans and others would say the same thing if they ever really read it. But though it is challenging, *it is the standard for citizens of heaven,* and we commit to live it because we believe the Kingdom of God has broken into history in Jesus, and we have made a solemn commitment before God to live it. It may be hard to live, but we believe that God is giving us the Holy Spirit and the power to do it (Luke 11:13).

3. And finally it means living as a kingdom of priests. We began this study in the second book of the Bible, seeing that God wanted his people to be a kingdom of priests. We conclude this chapter going to the last book of the Bible where we find this statement:

> To him who loves us and has freed us from our sins by his blood, and has made us to be a kingdom and priests to serve his God and Father—to him be glory and power for ever and ever! Amen. (Revelation 1:5b–6)

To this we can add Peter's well-known words:

> But you are a chosen people, a royal priesthood, a holy nation, a people belonging to God, that you may declare the praises of him who called you out of darkness into his wonderful light. Once you were not a people, but now you are the people of God; once you had not received mercy, but now you have received mercy.
>
> Dear friends, I urge you, as aliens and strangers in the world, to abstain from sinful desires, which war against your soul. (1 Peter 2:9–11)

Peter describes a new people and a new nation who belong to God and whose identity supersedes all other identities, and this nation is also a "royal priesthood" (or literally a kingdom priesthood). It is not a nation *with* a priesthood. The nation *is* the royal priesthood.

In our lives and our churches we need to be practicing the priesthood of all believers and thinking through how to apply this in various ways. Surely these ideas describe only a beginning:

- Going back to the Old Testament, certainly the key role of a priest was to bring others to God. That leads to every disciple having an evangelistic heart.
- We can see a correlation between the priestly role that each of us has with the great New Testament emphasis on being involved in "one another's" lives,

helping each other to stay faithful to the King and the Kingdom.[13]

- It surely means having no distinction between clergy and laity. "Clergy" comes from a word that means "priest." "Laity" comes from a word which means "people." *In the Kingdom all the people are the priests and all the priests are the people.* This, of course, does not set aside the idea of specialization of roles (as in Ephesians 4:11) or for some to receive church support because of devoting all their time to ministry work (1 Timothy 5:17).

- We saw with the Old Testament priests that they owned no land. It is obvious in the New Testament that this idea was not taught to Christians, but we do see in the New Testament a disenchantment with wealth and Jesus' teaching about not laying up treasures on earth. We see a willingness to part company with land and possessions to advance the kingdom cause (Acts 4:32–35).

- Finally, the priests did not fight. How does this fit with Jesus' words about non-resistance and loving one's enemies in Matthew 5 and Luke 6? What is the implication for us as a kingdom of priests?

To pray for God's Kingdom to come is to pray that we might live a kingdom life, not just have hope for future intervention. It is not praying about something that might happen *some* day, but to pray about what will happen in your life *this* day.

△

While Jesus never gave a definition of the Kingdom, it is clear that in him it arrived. From his teaching we also can see many powerful and life-changing perspectives regarding it. We can indeed know a lot about it. Earlier we used the Allied invasion on D-Day as an illustration. We have heard it said that after day one of that invasion, little had changed. But in another sense everything had changed, and it was then just a matter of time. A war that had been going on in Europe for five years would end in less than a year. D-Day was the beginning of the end.

When Jesus broke into history and brought the Kingdom of God with him, very little changed, and yet everything had changed. It is just a matter of time for this to be clear. The Apocalypse of John anticipates the consummation: "The kingdom of this world has become the kingdom of our Lord and of his Christ, and he will reign for ever and ever" (Revelation 11:15). The question for us is: Will we be humble *in it now* (and blessed in it now) or humbled *by it then* when it comes in all its fullness?

A favorite expression in our day seems to be "Now deal with it." "Okay, you married this person. Now deal with it." "That job is not coming back. Now deal with it." "You are having triplets. Now deal with it." Certainly with more care and compassion and with a much greater message of support, the New Testament is saying "In Jesus the future has broken in. Now deal with it. The age to come has arrived. Now be like it. Heaven has invaded earth. Now live it."

We will explore what it will take for today's disciples and today's church to do this in the next two chapters.

Questions for Study and Discussion

1. Why is it impossible to be in the Kingdom without repentance? Try to give an answer that includes more than "because God said so." Why would God say so?
2. In a similar way, why would it be impossible to live life in the Kingdom without a new birth from above?
3. Share about your own experiences of saying "The Lord's Prayer."
4. When did you really start praying in earnest that God's will be done in your life on earth as it is in heaven?
5. How does it affect your thinking to put more emphasis on "as it is in heaven"? Why does such a prayer lead to the Kingdom breaking in?
6. What are your thoughts about being a citizen of heaven who pledges ultimate allegiance to no kingdom except the Kingdom of God? What are the implications of this idea?
7. The authors believe we have applied too narrowly the charge of not being yoked with unbelievers. What are your thoughts?
8. Do you think the understanding that the church is not the same as the Kingdom diminishes the importance of the church or makes its role all the more important?

9. To live the kingdom life is to live as a disciple of Jesus, as a citizen of heaven, as a member of the kingdom of priests. Which of those do you connect with the most and why? Which one needs more attention in your life?

10. What difference will it make if we see the Kingdom not so much as an institution to maintain and be loyal to, but rather as a life to be lived?

NOTE: We include discussion questions at the end of each chapter, but they are also available on the web with permission to print and copy. (kingdombooks-vol1.blogspot.com)

4

The Kingdom Is Now

TODAY'S CHURCH LIVING THE KINGDOM LIFE

Part One

Once the resurrection of Jesus had taken place, there must have been a palpable sense among his disciples that more waves of the Kingdom were surely coming. But in his appearances to them, Jesus made it clear that the continual *coming* of the Kingdom would be closely tied to their *going* into the world to both share this good news and to live it out (Matthew 24:14, Matthew 28:18–19).

In this Stage One of a two-stage process, the coming of the Kingdom did not mean an end to normal life on earth. Instead it was the beginning of a time when the Kingdom would penetrate the world like salt and light and yeast through the lives of those who yielded themselves to the king. It meant they began living the age-to-come life even before that age arrived.

There were certain reasons they had for believing that Stage One might not go on for very long before the coming of Stage Two and the final consummation of the Kingdom. With Jesus' first appearing fresh in their minds, they had urgency about their mission in light of his coming back. However, the Scriptures are consistent in never predicting exactly when this will occur. It was understood that until this happened the church would bear witness to the Kingdom with its life, in word and deed.

What we want to examine in this chapter is what kind of people or church we need to be now so that the good news of God's in-breaking in Jesus and the Kingdom is demonstrated in our lives and is announced with our words. What we are talking about here is today's church living the kingdom life in a world that is no closer to living that life than the world of Jesus' time. We are also talking about the kind of people who will be the salt of the earth, preserving it from putrification, and the light of the world, giving those who will listen an opportunity to know the mystery of God revealed in Christ and the Kingdom.

People in Awe

It seems logical to begin with the fact that we need to be people in awe—in awe of the Kingdom and humbled by it. I (Tom) went to southern Colorado years ago and climbed to the top of the Wet Mountains. From there I looked across at the Sangre de Cristo range—a series of 14,000-foot peaks all taller than Pike's Peak. I stood in awe. The person who had spent most of his life in Alabama and Missouri and was getting his first view of the Rockies was stunned. That majestic view took away what little breath I still had and left me in awe.

The writer of Hebrews says in chapter 12:

> But you have come to Mount Zion, to the heavenly Jerusalem, the city of the living God. You have come to thousands upon thousands of angels in joyful assembly, to the church of the firstborn, whose names are written in heaven.... Therefore, since we are receiving a kingdom that cannot be shaken, let us be thankful, and so worship God acceptably with reverence and awe, for our "God is a consuming fire." (vv22–23a, 28–29)

We need to stand in awe of a plan that has been unfolding for centuries and that we know prophets longed to see. We need to be in awe of a reign that can touch the hearts of men and women from every culture and nation, and bring them together at one table and into one family. We need to stand in awe of the wisdom of God that accomplishes this in ways man would never imagine. We need to stand in awe of the cross and the dramatic truth that in this ugliest of human acts, the God of the towel is revealed, and the essence of the Kingdom is shown to be servanthood and sacrificial love.

We need to stand humbly in awe before the Kingdom— seeing it as God in the splendor of his "kingness," praying that it will more and more come to our hearts and minds, confessing that we have much to learn. We must be in awe of the one who rules the Kingdom, knowing that he alone knows its borders, its height and depth and breadth and width, and never pretending that we have a corner on it or have it all packaged and figured out.

It is the greatest of mistakes to equate the Kingdom with the church and then think that all we have to do is read the blueprint or pattern of the church—supposedly easy to find in the New Testament—and then have the Kingdom of God in a nice institutional form, easy to explain and easy to grasp. Those who do that do not stand in awe of such a kingdom. Why should they? They have it diagramed and explained with a printout of its members. They seem to have much more control over it than it has over them. We are not sure if God laughs or cries.

We have seen that the Kingdom is entered only with humility, but what we must understand is that if we think we have it all boxed up and under our control, we have just been ushered out the back door. To stay in the Kingdom requires awe and humility.

People Receiving

We learned in the aforementioned Hebrews 12:28— "We are receiving a kingdom…"—that the Kingdom is something to continue to receive. Remember the present active participle indicating continuing action. We must be a people never thinking we have arrived, never thinking we have somehow restored the Kingdom. Instead we must be a humble people ever open to God showing us new understandings and bringing the kingdom life to us in fresh ways. Kingdom people are most rare amongst religious persons. They are always asking "What is the kingdom thing to do here?" and then being completely open to thinking ways they have never thought before and doing things in ways they have never done them.

The two of us have seen just how powerful this approach can be. We have been in situations that looked all too familiar. There were conflicts in the fellowship, and our minds could flash back to how situations like these ended badly. But we are blessed to be part of a leadership group who is open to thinking in new ways and is willing to handle situations in adherence to kingdom principles. Following the principle in the Sermon on the Mount of an over-the-top kind of generosity and submissiveness, we have seen God bless us in special ways.

But not only do we need to be a people receiving more of the Kingdom, but also people continually receiving the Spirit, who gives us the power to live the kingdom life that is so alien to our flesh. In Ephesians 5:8, Paul writes: "Do not get drunk on wine, which leads to debauchery. Instead, be filled with the Spirit." It was famed writer John Stott who first called our attention to the Greek verb *pleroo*—"be filled"—in this verse. Tom summed up what we learned in his book on Ephesians:

> First, we need to notice that this verb is in *the imperative mood*. That means it is a command. The fullness of

God's Spirit is not an option for us. We can no more please the Lord without the Spirit of God in our lives than we can drive to work today without gas in our cars. Being filled with the Spirit is something essential and something about which we must be urgent. We will be filled with the Spirit or we will not belong to Christ. (See also Romans 8:9.)

Second, we need to notice that this is in *the plural form*, which means this is something for the whole church. Every child of God is to be filled with the Spirit. This is not just for leaders but for every disciple. But there is more. Already in Ephesians we have seen the connection between the Holy Spirit and the body of Christ. The temple of the Holy Spirit is not just individual Christians in isolation from each other; rather the temple of the Spirit is the body of Christ. We will not be filled with the Spirit if we are disconnected from one another. Being filled with the Spirit is something that happens to us together with our brothers and sisters. Sure, we all need times alone with God, and yes, those times can be spiritually filling, but we will not maintain what we have found without fellowship. The verb is plural.

Third, we need to notice that this verb is in *the passive voice*. The sentence does not read, "Fill yourself with the Spirit," but "Be filled with the Spirit." We cannot work hard enough to make this happen, but here is what we can do: We can be open and receptive, and we can allow Christ to fill us with the Spirit. We can admit our need and come before him in humility, asking him to put in us what we cannot find on our own. Some of us try to psyche ourselves up. We talk ourselves into taking action. That may work for a while and fool a few people here and there, but it is not the same as humbly opening our lives and allowing God to fill us with his Spirit.

Finally, we must note that this exhortation is in *the present tense*. Had Paul wanted to communicate that this filling of the Holy Spirit was something that happens only once at a definite point in time, he could have used the aorist tense in Greek. But he chose the present tense, which in a context like this one carries with it the idea of *continuous action.*

In other words he is saying, "Keep on being filled with the Spirit" or "Be filled with the Spirit again and again." Certainly we were all given the gift of the Spirit at our baptism (Acts 2:38) and that only happens once, but again and again we must let the Spirit fill us with his fruit, his conviction and his renewing power. The days are evil and the world has a way of wearing us all down. Again and again, we must come back to God and his people and allow ourselves to be filled with the Spirit.

There is one last thing to say about this verb, and you don't have to know grammar to see this one. The word "filled" speaks for itself. Paul is calling for us to let the Spirit permeate every area of our lives. Being filled doesn't mean being somewhat filled or partially filled. It means just what it looks like it means—filled![1]

The Kingdom is something we keep on receiving and the Spirit is something we need to keep on receiving. There is great interplay between the two.

- The challenges of the kingdom life reveal to us our need for the Spirit.
- The Spirit works in us and in the fellowship to open our eyes to more of the Kingdom's call than we have seen.
- The Spirit then gives us the power and strength to live that call.

The Kingdom calls for us to seek it first, and the Spirit then works to guide us when we cry out, "God, our Father, what is your will here?"

People in Prayer

It makes perfect sense that Jesus' teaching on the Kingdom was interspersed with teaching on prayer. It is logical that Jesus would have two sections on prayer in the Sermon on the Mount. It stands to reason that the church in Acts—those commissioned to carry the message of the Kingdom—would constantly be turning to prayer. If we are putting ourselves under the rule and reign of God, we obviously need a consistent connection to him. Consider at least three other reasons that kingdom people must be people in prayer.

First, living this life is so different from what we are naturally that only a continuing connection with God will enable us to live it.

Often without the "prayer of examine"—"Search me, O God, and know my heart.... Lead me in the way everlasting"—we will not even hear certain truths that Jesus taught.

We will read right over them and miss the point. It took a new birth from above to start us on this journey, and it will take continuing connection from above to keep us on it.

Second, kingdom teaching will sometimes baffle us.

Jesus will say something such as "Do not resist an evil person," and our minds immediately shift into "Surely, he doesn't mean this or mean that." We end up confused. At a loss, we may just avoid such teaching or call it a disputable matter. But in the Sermon on the Mount, Jesus has just the word for us:

> "Ask and it will be given to you; seek and you will find; knock and the door will be opened to you. For everyone who asks receives; he who seeks finds; and to him who knocks, the door will be opened.
> "Which of you, if his son asks for bread, will give him a stone? Or if he asks for a fish, will give him a snake? If you, then, though you are evil, know how to give good gifts to your children, how much more will your Father in heaven give good gifts to those who ask him! So in everything, do to others what you would have them do to you, for this sums up the Law and the Prophets." (Matthew 7:7–12)

Earlier we said the three most important words in biblical interpretation are context, context, context. What is the context of this statement? The Sermon on the Mount and the kingdom life. Jesus gives the teaching in this context. It seems to us that the first place to apply this is to ask, seek and knock for an understanding of how to live out Jesus' commands. Surely Jesus understands that people seeking to live this age-to-come life in the present age are going to run into some problems, and he calls us to believing prayer.

If, I (Steve) who am fluent in Spanish and have spent much time in Latin America, were to take Tom along on one of my trips, getting around on his three-wheeled scooter in a third-world country might be the least of Tom's troubles. He would be in a very different world. Communication in another language and culture would bring challenges and questions. And so with us in the Kingdom.

But what are we to do when we encounter problems and times of confusion as we seek to live by the standards of another world? We are to pray: to ask, to seek, to knock. And anytime we come with an open heart, wanting to do the Father's will on earth as it is in heaven, he will not mock our prayers but will lead us to the answers. No, not always to the answers we may have hoped for but to something better: the truth—his truth. It is sad when disciples get wrought up about some teaching of Jesus, defensively react, and never stop to pray for the openness and humility needed to receive guidance.

What do we ask for? Not health, or wealth, or status, but wisdom and power to see the Kingdom clearly and live the Kingdom fully—to receive the Kingdom, to sit down at the banquet table that is the Kingdom.

Is the kingdom life compatible with an entertainment career in today's world, with a big house and a big yacht, with even a nice middle-class home, with a retirement account, with political positions in government, with the military?

Some of these may have a place or they may not. How much have we prayed for answers? How much have we prayed with others about these things? How much have we asked others to keep praying for us to find truth?

Third, prayer is so essential because we will be opposed by spiritual forces, other people and forces within us.

It is an enormous challenge. As we have seen, the colony of heaven will not always be welcomed. Author Lee Camp quotes Richard Hays who said: "[In Christ] we become the righteousness of God. The church incarnates the righteousness of God." And then Camp adds: "For this reason, the church will often be in trouble."[2]

"If they persecuted me, they will persecute you, also" said Jesus (John 15:20). How will you handle it when you take a stand on a kingdom principle, and your little son comes home and says, "Johnny's parents say we must be in a cult" or "They say we are weird because we don't believe in…"? Persecution is a hard thing even if it is just in the form of social pressure or ostracism. Jesus said it would be *inevitable* for kingdom people. When persecuted, Jesus prayed. When persecuted, the early church prayed. We will not handle it well without prayer. We cannot live this full but challenging life without walking with the Father, the Son and the Holy Spirit.

When the two of us first began to talk some about our study of the Kingdom, a friend of ours said, "I think I need to go to Academy Sports and buy me some knee pads because I am going to need to be on my knees a lot." He got it right.

"This, then, is how you should pray:
"'Our Father in heaven,
hallowed be your name,
your kingdom come,
your will be done
on earth as it is in heaven.'" (Matthew 6:9–10)

People Trusting

When the one who brings the Kingdom and the one who embodies the Kingdom talks repeatedly about faith and about trusting him and the Father, you know it is vital to the whole enterprise. When his message is examined closely, what Jesus is concerned about people having is not a general faith in God, but a faith that God was at work in him bringing the new age and that his words can be trusted. He was amazed when he did not find that faith in Israel, and he was amazed when he did find it in a Roman centurion. He frequently admonished people for their little faith and affirmed those who demonstrated great faith.

The importance of this kind of faith is seen in Jesus' statement from Luke 18:8: "I tell you, he will see that they get justice, and quickly. However, when the Son of Man comes, will he find faith on the earth?" When Jesus returns to bring in the Kingdom with all its fullness, what he will be looking for is faith on the earth. He will be looking for those who trusted him—not in some compartmentalized way in which we say "I trusted Jesus for my salvation" and then live like we trust ourselves for everything else. No, he will be looking for those who believed his agenda was right and "sold the farm," if you will, "left all," surrendered their agenda and put everything under his reign. This is about people who turned to him in repentance, trusting that God would be at work in this strange age-to-come lifestyle.

Jesus says some things that sound strange to our culture. He is not a bland teacher of moral platitudes who was loved by everyone. As Stanley Hauweras puts it, "Jesus was not crucified for saying and doing what made sense to everyone."[3] Following him is a counter-cultural move. No inherited cultural belief or alliance with civil religion will give a people the gumption or the guts to obey him. No, it will take a deep conviction that he is the One from God and that his way of sacrifice and the cross is the right one, and all his promises are true.

Kingdom people will constantly be looking at what appears to be long odds against them and deciding that regardless, Jesus is the one to trust. When the kingdom life seems to stretch them too far, they will learn from those in the Gospels to cry out, "Lord, increase our faith" (Luke 17:5) or "I do believe; help me overcome my unbelief" (Mark 9:24). As Habakkuk wrote and Paul quoted: "The righteous will live by faith" (Habakkuk 2:4, Romans 1:17).

People with Confidence

While kingdom people will live with humility, they also must live with confidence. God's Kingdom will have no impressive earthly credentials—no stealth bombers, battleships or aircraft carriers, no shining capitol building and no trillion dollar budget. It will be given no seat at the United Nations. It will have no team in the Olympics and no team at the World Cup. Unlike its precursor—the nation of Israel—the Kingdom of God does not even have a beautiful temple and the dramatic pageantry and sights and sounds (and smells!) that made worship seem so real. Amidst the much ado and pomp of the world, even in the religious world, Christians may feel intimidated or even a bit embarrassed that they follow one known as "the lamb that was slain" and preach a wisdom that seems like foolishness to the scholars and philosophers of this age.

There is evidence from the New Testament letters that both of these sentiments were being felt in the first-century churches. We have referred twice to Hebrews 12:28. To those converts from Judaism who may have wanted something more impressive, the writer reminds them that we have a kingdom that cannot be shaken. That conviction and the confidence it gives seems to permeate the entire letter. "...if we hold firmly till the end the confidence we had at first" (3:14), "...we have confidence" (10:19), "So do not throw away your confidence" (10:35), and "So we say with confidence, 'The Lord is my helper; I will not be afraid. What can man do to me?'" (13:6).

This confidence is based on nothing that normally causes it—not physical force or beauty, not ancestry, not degrees, not personality, and certainly not wealth, privilege or majority status. *It is all based on the man Jesus.* Paul's words are almost a commentary on Hebrews: "Such confidence as this is ours through Christ before God" (2 Corinthians 3:4). The writer of Hebrews begins to paint the picture of Jesus with these words that open his letter:

> In the past God spoke to our forefathers through the prophets at many times and in various ways, but

> in these last days he has spoken to us by his Son, whom he appointed heir of all things, and through whom he made the universe. The Son is the radiance of God's glory and the exact representation of his being, sustaining all things by his powerful word. After he had provided purification for sins, he sat down at the right hand of the Majesty in heaven. (Hebrews 1:1–3)

This Kingdom cannot be shaken because it comes from the one who created us and then provided the way for us to be recreated. He is the one who tasted death for everyone (2:9), was made perfectly fit for that role through what he suffered (2:10), is not ashamed to call us brothers (2:11), sympathizes with our weaknesses (4:15), and gives us confidence to come to the throne of grace (4:16).

The church is called to proclaim an out-of-this-world, age-to-come message. It will seem to some not only out of the box but off the wall, but we must proclaim it with confidence, knowing, to return to Daniel's prophecy, that all other kingdoms have feet of clay; only the one brought by Jesus will endure forever. As our writer of Hebrews puts it, "In putting everything under him, God left nothing that is not subject to him. Yet at present we do not see everything subject to him. But we see Jesus…" (2:8–9a). The church does not need the latest method, a course in cutting-edge leadership, or a wealthy and generous disciple. The church needs a confidence that comes from being captivated by a clear vision of Jesus, who according to our writer is "the same yesterday and today and forever" (Hebrews 13:8).

People Obeying

In the eight Beatitudes that begin his Sermon on the Kingdom, Jesus made it clear that the kingdom life is not first of all about *doing*, but about *being*. This is where we must start—with attitudes of the heart. Unless we grasp "poor in spirit," we have little chance of not judging. Unless we understand "meek," we will chaff at "don't resist an evil person." Unless we have the "hunger and thirst for righteousness," seeking the Kingdom first will be a battle, and not storing up "treasures on earth" will be an imposition. Unless we seek "merciful," we will balk at "forgive seventy-seven times." Unless we pray for a "pure heart," loving our enemies will be overcome by nationalism or patriotism.

But while the Sermon starts with the focus on *being*, soon one realizes that Jesus' kingdom teaching is not about a vague journey into an ontological fog. It is about being new people who obey the Lord who has graciously invited us to his banquet table. While the Sermon begins focused on *being*, it definitely ends focused on *doing*—particularly on obeying:

> "Not everyone who says to me, 'Lord, Lord,' will enter the kingdom of heaven, but only he who does *the will of my Father* who is in heaven. Many will say to me on that day, 'Lord, Lord, did we not prophesy in your name, and in your name drive out demons and perform many miracles?' Then I will tell them plainly, 'I never knew you. Away from me, you evildoers!'

"Therefore everyone who hears these words of mine and *puts them into practice* is like a wise man who built his house on the rock." (Matthew 7:21–24, emphasis added)

Those who are known by Jesus as citizens of his Kingdom are those who hear his words and put them into practice. In every era, when believers were focused on kingdom living, they were almost always drawn to the Sermon on the Mount and had a heart to obey it. They understood that for the Kingdom to be present in our world, for the Kingdom to be something that is "now," disciples cannot be committed to a vague kind of believism, but must be specifically and purposefully committed to a kingdom life, particularly as Jesus describes it in the Sermon on the Mount.

True followers of Jesus will not dismiss the Sermon on the Mount as "impossible" or argue that it was "only for the apostles" and not for ordinary Christians. In addition they will not see it as something that just makes us aware of our need for grace, although it does that quite powerfully. Jesus could not be clearer: He expects his followers to obey and to live his message. This is exactly what grace teaches us to do (Titus 2:11–12).

We cannot be serious about making disciples who will obey everything that Jesus commanded if we do not give special attention to this text. Let us encourage this exercise: Read through the Sermon on the Mount, marking every teaching (1) that you hear very little about, or (2) that you do not seriously apply to your life. Make a list of what you find, and start talking to others about these and praying about a new emphasis in your fellowship on these teachings of Jesus that we must obey.

In the next book in this series, we plan to go carefully through the Sermon. Here we just say that people's commitment to search it out, pray over it, and courageously obey it, will show whether they want to live the Kingdom or just want to shape their own version of it, contradicting its basic premise—total submission to the will of our king.

Whatever we do, we must not come to Jesus' most radical and challenging teaching looking for reasons *not* to obey or for a way to talk something into the ground until we feel comfortable just ignoring it. Our first response to Jesus' kingdom teachings should not be, "Surely it doesn't mean this" or "It can't mean this." We must come with a heart that is eager to obey, and seeks, and asks, and knocks until we find a way to obey.

Maybe there have been times when you were so grateful to someone and so eager to please them that obeying some request was a joy and no burden at all. That is what putting on Jesus' good yoke should be about. But even in such a situation, we can be asked to do something that doesn't seem to fit with who we naturally are. Though we want to respond, something causes internal conflict. In seeking to obey Jesus, then, it should not surprise us that we will go through quite a struggle with some issues. After all, we were raised in this present age, and now we are receiving an in-breaking, age-to-come culture.

Let's look at an example that highlights the emotional struggles we will sometimes face in the arena of obedience.

Suppose you were trained in martial arts from an early age. Partly it was for the sport and the discipline, but your father was a major advocate of self defense. It was drilled into you as a basic right. But then you read the kingdom way: "Do not resist an evil person. If someone strikes you on the right cheek, turn to him the other also" (Matthew 5:39). Thoughts about this stir up powerful emotions. You aren't sure how to obey. It stops you in your tracks.

But let's offer another example that is closer to home for us. Both of us are fathers of several children. While we have never been enamored by material things, we still have thought a good deal about providing for our families and having something for our retirement years so we are not a burden to anyone. We can hear the words of our fathers who grew up in the depression, cautioning us to hold on to our money. But then Jesus comes with his kingdom message: "Do not store up for yourselves treasures on earth, where moth and rust destroy, and where thieves break in and steal (Matthew 6:19)...but seek first [God's] kingdom..." (6:33).

What should one do? This is over-simplified, but consider several guidelines: (1) Don't say "Surely, he doesn't mean..." (2) Have an honest-with-God prayer time. (3) Whatever you say in that prayer time (and it is fine to get it all out), end it with "But, Father, it spite of all these thoughts and feelings, I really want to do your will. Help me see it and do it." (4) Have some honest time with a spiritually mature person who will help you find ways to obey. (5) Read and pray through Psalm 119 to cultivate an obedient heart. (6) If you are afraid to obey, remember the confidence we have because of Jesus and surrender your fear. (7) Take action; baby steps are fine; avoidance is not. Do not ignore this matter and just hope it goes away.

Whatever it takes, we must get to obedience. Go through Bunyan's Slough of Despond, go through the desert of struggle, but keep going until you get to obedience. It is not enough for us to declare that the Kingdom has come or to tell others about the keys. We must show the Kingdom. This was the power of Jesus' ministry: He proclaimed the Kingdom and called people to it, but all the while he was living the kingdom life. When you look at him you see what it looks like for a human being to be consumed by the Kingdom. "Are you really the one or should we look for someone else?" asked John the Baptist through a messenger, showing us his own humanity and tendency to doubt. And then we read:

> Jesus replied, "Go back and report to John what you hear and see: The blind receive sight, the lame walk, those who have leprosy are cured, the deaf hear, the dead are raised, and the good news is preached to the poor. Blessed is the man who does not fall away on account of me." (Matthew 11:4–6)

Jesus' life was the confirmation of the message. He was about the business of the Kingdom. Jesus showed the Kingdom by fulfilling the Law and the Prophets. We show the Kingdom by standing before Jesus' words with an obedient heart, a heart eager to act. Claiborne and Haw, speaking of the early church, have captured well this spirit:

Making disciples meant that they were teaching the world to do the things that Jesus did: to wash feet, to proclaim jubilee, to love enemies, to welcome strangers. (And they would become known as the Way.) Their community was more than a group of people who shared religious beliefs. They were a group of people that embodied a new way of living—the way out of the empire, where slavery, poverty, war, oppression were normal. They were to become the salt and the light of the world. *The credibility of their gospel would rest on the integrity of their lives* [emphasis added].[4]

No one can have credibility with the gospel of the Kingdom without a passion for obedience. Of course, the concern here is not how high one scores on an obedience test, but how eagerly one desires to obey with a hunger and thirst for righteousness. With this attitude, we will want to do the will of God without trying to figure out exactly what will happen if we obey. Lee Camp warns us of the danger:

"Effectiveness" or "realistic expectations" of "whatever is safe" or "whatever is necessary"—all these catchphrases subtly rely upon a calculation of intended results, trusting that human wisdom can determine the best course of action, even if it means setting aside faithful witness to the ways of the kingdom.[5]

We must come to Jesus' message with a single-minded desire to obey. We must not come calculating how "effective" obedience may be or asking if it will really "work." The way of the cross may never look "effective" to the world, and by the world's calculations, maybe it never "works," but it must be enough for us that Jesus calls us to it.

In chapter 5 we will continue to examine qualities the church and each of us must have if we are to live the kingdom life, and then we will call for some self-evaluation.

Questions for Study and Discussion

1. Do you believe people in our day can live the kingdom life? What will be the challenges?

2. What do we need to grasp in order to be in the Kingdom with a sense of awe? What hinders this response?

3. What are the implications of the truth that we need to keep on receiving the Kingdom?

4. How is continuing to receive the Kingdom connected with continuing to be filled with the Spirit? Why must they stay together in our lives?

5. In his Sermon on the Kingdom Jesus includes two major sections on prayer. The authors give three reasons prayer is so essential to the kingdom life. Which one do you identify with the most and why?

6. Both faith and confidence are discussed in this chapter. How would you describe the relationship between them? What for you brings a strengthening in these two areas?

7. What did you learn by doing the exercise the authors proposed concerning the Sermon on the Mount? What is one area you want to seriously seek to obey?

8. How is obedience related to the challenge given by Lee Camp not to focus on what is "effective" or "what is safe" or "what is necessary"?

9. What is your view of the seven steps offered for dealing with a command of Jesus that "stops you in your tracks"?
10. How would you describe the different understandings you are grasping about the Kingdom in this study?

NOTE: We include discussion questions at the end of each chapter, but they are also available on the web with permission to print and copy. (kingdombooks-vol1.blogspot.com)

5

The Kingdom Is Now

TODAY'S CHURCH LIVING THE KINGDOM LIFE

Part Two

Having considered in the last chapter six vital qualities the church must have to embody the Kingdom in today's world, we now will consider three more. Of course, there are many more than these nine, but it is our conviction that responding to these will lead us to other places we need to go.

People in Community

While we narrow the scope of the Kingdom by identifying it simply as the church, the place you go to find a mother lode of kingdom thinking should be the church. As we have seen, the church is not the same as the Kingdom, but the church is the fellowship of those who have received the Kingdom and keep receiving the Kingdom. It is the place on earth where one should find the age to come breaking into the present age. In fact, if you don't find it in the church, you will not find it anywhere else. And wherever you find people devoted to the Kingdom, there you have the church. It is *Plan A* in Jesus' strategy, and there is no *Plan B* because he does not intend to let *Plan A* fail (Matthew 16:18).

If you find someone who says, "I am just going to be an independent kingdom person because the church has done nothing but distort the real Kingdom," we suggest that you not ridicule them. They have an emotional reaction to some truly bad things that have been done. Show them some kingdom-style mercy as you guide them to various texts, including the one just cited in Matthew 16. Then guide them through the seven steps we described in chapter 4 for those who struggle emotionally with obedience.

God's plan has always been to have a people, a community, a network, and not multiple individuals who are disconnected from each other. After the wave of the Kingdom came in the power of the Spirit on Pentecost, three thousand experienced new birth through repentance and baptism. Filled with the Holy Spirit, "they devoted themselves to the apostles teaching and to the fellowship, to the breaking of bread and to prayer" (Acts 2:43).

Here the KJV says "They continued steadfastly...in the fellowship." The word is *proskartereo* and has to do with diligence and earnestness. The word for "fellowship," of course, is one of most beautiful of Greek words—*koinonia*. At its root is the idea of a shared life. It comes from the word *koinos* which means "common." No one English word really translates *koinonia*. It is rendered "fellowship" in Acts 2, "partnership" in Philippians 1, and "participation" (or "communion") in 1 Corinthians 11. Perhaps the best translation of the word is found in the New English Bible: "sharing together in the common life."[1] It is all about togetherness, sharing and living a life in common.

Typically people in religion are focused on their individual salvation as in: "I just want to go to heaven when I die. I just want to be sure my relationship with God is right. It is just me and God!" Even a beautiful song like "My God and I" can reinforce such thinking. Notice the last two lines:

> This earth will pass, and with it common trifles,
> But God and I will go unendingly.

Often someone will tell us about their membership in a certain church. When one of us asks, "Oh, I suppose you have some people there who are really involved in your life?" it is remarkable how often the answer is "No, not really." That is the way of mainstream religion, but the biblical emphasis is on people being part of the community doing the will of God *together* as a people—people involved in one another's lives, helping one another to seek God's will on earth as it is in heaven.

We return again to a text from Isaiah:

> See, a king will reign in righteousness
> and rulers will rule with justice.

Each man will be like a shelter from the wind
    and a refuge from the storm,
like streams of water in the desert
    and the shadow of a great rock in a thirsty land.
(Isaiah 32:1–2)

In the Kingdom, people will be together and will be there for each other. As we seek the Kingdom, that is, as we seek to live the kingdom life, that is, as we seek to live the Sermon on the Mount and other kingdom teachings of Jesus, let us say it loud and clear: *We need one another.* We need to be involved in one another's lives and seeking the Kingdom first *together.* To do this individually is self-contradictory. In the age to come we will not be by ourselves. There will be no hermits, monks, Lone Rangers or rugged individualists. So, when the age to come breaks into the present age right now, what you see is people "sharing together in the common life."

This *koinonia* plays several key roles in connection with the Kingdom:[2]

First, it is where we initially put into practice kingdom living.

Returning to Isaiah, we see that it is in the community where natural enemies come together in a peaceable Kingdom.

The cow will feed with the bear,
    their young will lie down together,
    and the lion will eat straw like the ox....

They will neither harm nor destroy
    on all my holy mountain,

> for the earth will be full of the knowledge of the Lord
> as the waters cover the sea. (Isaiah 11:7, 9)

We can well remember when friends of ours planted an inter-racial church in South Africa just as apartheid was ending. Before long, an Afrikaner policeman had become a follower of Jesus in a fellowship that was at least 50 percent black. He came out of his baptism to leave his old life—and *whole* life—of prejudice behind. We remember the photos of him with black brothers who had once been jailed unfairly.

I (Steve) think particularly of Bogotá, Colombia, where former right-wing paramilitary members sit down at the Lord's Table with those who were left-wing guerrillas. The Kingdom is where we come together from all backgrounds, resolve conflicts, forgive each other and lay down our lives for each other (Matthew 5:23–24, John 13:34–35, 1 John 3:16).

Kingdom people practice kingdom love for all men, even for their enemies, but the place where this self-sacrificing love is demonstrated most intensely with a high degree of reciprocity is in the fellowship of the believers.

Second, the fellowship is where we get needed support and encouragement.

We are living this kingdom life in a world rebellious toward God and often hostile toward citizens of the Kingdom—this wears on us. In his letter to the churches, Peter spoke early and often of their status as misfits in the culture of this world:

- Peter, an apostle of Jesus Christ, To God's elect, strangers in the world, scattered throughout Pontus, Galatia, Cappadocia, Asia and Bithynia…(1 Peter 1:1)
- Since you call on a Father who judges each man's work impartially, live your lives as strangers here in reverent fear. (1 Peter 1:17)
- Dear friends, I urge you, as aliens and strangers in the world, to abstain from sinful desires, which war against your soul. (1 Peter 2:11)
- For you have spent enough time in the past doing what pagans choose to do—living in debauchery, lust, drunkenness, orgies, carousing and detestable idolatry. They think it strange that you do not plunge with them into the same flood of dissipation, and they heap abuse on you. (1 Peter 4:3–4)

In this world we are foreigners and aliens and strangers ("aliens from the future," says a friend of ours). Add in the derisive monikers of oddballs, misfits and religious nuts, and you have the picture. The earth is really ours and ultimately we will inherit it (Matthew 5:5). But for now it is occupied territory, and those in control will find us strange. There is no call here for us to try to act odd—no need for strange clothes or unfashionable haircuts. There is just a call for us to seek the Kingdom. That alone will set us apart.

What we are writing about will make little sense to those whose religion seems to blend seamlessly into the culture so that they experience little in the way of hostile reactions. However, those committed to the radically different age-to-come life will connect and understand. We have already experienced the way the world beats on us, even as we war against our own flesh. But God has provided us a fellowship where we encourage, support and inspire each other to fight the spiritual battles with "weapons of righteousness in the right hand and left" (2 Corinthians 6:7) and where we urge each other on to "finish the race" (Acts 20:24). If there is little conflict between our message and values and those of the world around us, we should wonder just how much of a kingdom life we are living. Kingdom-seekers will feel like aliens.

We may catch our own share of critique for this analogy, but the church's life in this world is more like the TV series *Lost* than like the Tom Hanks movie *Cast Away*. In both cases an airline crash sets up the storyline with the characters on remote South Pacific islands. In the movie, the Hanks character is totally alone after the FedEx plane he was catching a ride on goes down. His only friend is a volleyball named…what else? *Wilson*. It says so right there on one of the panels. The Hanks character is in hostile territory, and he has to manage all alone.

In the TV series *Lost* there are a number of survivors. They soon realize that dark forces are at work against them. Their best strategy is to work together, employing their diversity of talents and supporting each other, which they do with varying degrees of success. We did not watch the whole series, but the final episode seemed to depict most of the main characters getting to "heaven" together. Interesting.

Hanks' remarkable acting in *Cast Away*, and especially his portrayal of his relationship with Wilson, said loudly, to us anyway, that we are not meant to fight the battles alone. We will even start a relationship with a volleyball to overcome our aloneness. Even if the writers did not intend to send this "kingdom message," it is certainly true that living the kingdom life was never to be done alone.

It is significant that the prayer in the middle of the Sermon, begins, "Our Father," not "My Father," and it continues, asking for "our" daily bread and for forgiveness of "our" debts (trespasses). N.T. Wright and others have pointed out that the whole idea of "my personal relationship with God" apart from the community is a modern innovation.

Third, in the fellowship we learn from each other.

Earlier we compared the Kingdom to a great mountain that we might drive around and view from different angles. The beauty of the fellowship is that Steve may see things that Tom misses, but Tom sees things Steve didn't catch, and our friends may see things neither one of us saw. In this regard we find Paul's instruction to Philemon quite interesting: "I pray that you may be active in sharing your faith, so that you will have a full understanding of every good thing we have in Christ" (Philemon 6).

Many have used this to encourage people to evangelize, but the word here for sharing is again our word *koinonia* which almost always refers to Christians interacting with each other. As we together seek this kingdom life, different ones of us will become convicted about different areas and then set the pace in that area, showing the rest of us things we need to learn. We can easily hear Paul telling Philemon to "fellowship his faith" (so rendered in Young's translation). In our own fellowshipping of kingdom faith, we have learned from several brothers about caring for the poor while making disciples, from another the power of obedience in driving the speed limit (we aren't kidding!), and from others God's heart for orphans.

As we seek the Kingdom and fight the spiritual battles, God has given us a fellowship, a place to share together in the common life, and it is good.

People Telling

Like the earliest church, we find ourselves still living between the times. The Kingdom has come. We have entered it. We keep receiving it. We have given up our sovereignty and have submitted to the reign of God. We have tasted the powers of the age to come. We have been given the picture of what it is like to live God's will on earth as it is in heaven. Now Jesus calls us to go into all nations and tell the good news of the Kingdom.

Having come this far in our examination of the Kingdom, let's look at a familiar passage, prayerfully with fresh eyes. Speaking to that first little fellowship of disciples, Jesus makes the following statements in chapter 28 of Matthew.

> "All authority in heaven and on earth has been given to me."

Jesus is Lord. He is the Lord of the *now* and the *not yet*. He is the Lord of the present age *and* the age to come. As Paul will later say, "God placed all things under his feet" (Ephesians 1:22) and "he is before all things, and in him all things hold together" (Colossians 1:17). Here is a holy nation you can commit to because here is a leader who will not leave office because of a scandal. Here is a servant king whose reign is eternal.

> "Therefore, go and make disciples of all nations."

The church does not exist for itself. The fellowship is not to be selfishly enjoyed. Just as the prophets envisioned it, the Kingdom is to go to all nations, and we are to take it there. Literally, the Greek text could be translated "As you go, disciple the nations (*ta ethne*—'all ethnic groups')." It almost sounds like he had already given the disciples an expectation of going. Perhaps being with him for three years had caused them to understand: "Well, of course, we have to go because this story must be told. God has broken in but not as we expected. What looked like tragedy was really a victory. The Kingdom has arrived. We are standing here looking at him. Aren't we?" (v17). Now we are to help others learn what we have learned.

> "Baptizing them in the name of the Father and of the Son and of the Holy Spirit..."

The phrase "in the name of" has a background story. Some of us may recall it showing up in some old movies, as in "Stop in the name of the law." This more "contemporary" usage is a bit like its ancient predecessor. Scholars have found that there was a slight difference in the way it was used in Hebrew culture and in Greek culture. Among those in Hebrew culture it meant "with respect to," "to be set in relationship to," "for the sake of," or "to be attached to." In Greek culture it was more the idea of "to be appropriated by," "to belong to," "to submit to," "to be dedicated to." Of the two the Hebrew understanding certainly was warmer and had a more relational sound.

Since Jesus was Jewish, perhaps we should think, "I baptize you in respect of the Father, for the sake of the Son, to be attached to the Holy Spirit, and so you might be in relationship with the Father, the Son and the Holy Spirit." But if we wanted to add "So you belong to God, have submitted to the Lordship of the Son, and will have the seal of ownership placed on you by the Holy Spirit," we would most likely still be on track.

Baptism is not mechanical; it is relational. One should be baptized only because he or she is ready to be shaped by fellowship with God. And so, no wonder Paul would say we are "baptized into Christ." We are united with him in baptism. We are buried with him and raised with him. We are clothed with him. We put him on. We make him our life.

> "...and teaching them to obey everything I have commanded you."

We must not pick and choose. We must not leave out the hard stuff. We must teach others everything. Why not start with the Sermon? It is all about the Kingdom. It is Jesus' Kingdom Manifesto. But then we aren't just transferring information; we are teaching people to obey. The first element in teaching, of course, is demonstration. To teach obedience we must be living obedience.

> "And surely I am with you always, to the very end of the age."

To "disciple" the people will be hard work. To bring them to baptism will be challenging—if we are doing a thorough job. To teach them to obey everything? Sounds more than difficult. Sounds impossible. But then this promise: He will be with us all the way through this present age, to the very end, when he will usher us into the fullness of the new age.

As kingdom people, we are a commissioned people. We are a holy nation and a royal priesthood that is to tell the world of things too wonderful to describe. We have found a treasure in a field. We have discovered a pearl of incredible value. We have been invited to a great feast. And the world needs to know. Our neighbors and family need to know. Our enemies need to know because all that is ours can also be theirs.

People of Courage

This kingdom life is not religion as usual. This is not American civil religion. This is not Sunday religion. This is not entertainer's religion. This is not touchdown religion.

This is not foxhole religion. This is not emergency room religion. This is not God & Country religion. This is not Christmas-Easter-weddings-funerals religion. This probably isn't even religion at all—at least the way most people think of religion. This is more like entering one of the parallel universes some cosmologists talk about as part of string theory. This is entering a new order of life. This is a new nation, a new citizenship, and new loyalties with a new perspective on everything. This is what Paul describes in 2 Corinthians 5:17. Look at the passage in three translations.

> So then, if anyone is in Christ, he is a new creation; what is old has passed away—look, what is new has come! (NET)

> What this means is that those who become Christians become new persons. They are not the same anymore, for the old life is gone. A new life has begun! (NLT)

> So if any man is in Christ, he is in a new world: the old things have come to an end; they have truly become new. (BBE)

This clearly says that we will be different. And since this new life that is characterized by self-sacrificing love exposes the old life for what it is just by its very existence, new kingdom people will be different in ways that are often not welcomed. This leads to our last characteristic.

For the church today to be an embodiment of the Kingdom, it must be people courageous—a people with the courage to preach differently and live differently. People with the courage to be sacrificial and to be stigmatized and to be strangers in this world. People with the courage to be open to new ideas that are really just neglected ideas long ago taught by Jesus. People with the courage to go where we have not gone before and to live what we have not lived before…if that is where Jesus' message calls us to go.

Years ago one of us was in a church that was making an impact on the community. Many were coming to the cross from the campuses and from the city, and predictably, opposition was coming to the believers. An elder said, "I don't like this. I have been a Christian for twenty years and have never been persecuted, and I don't want it to start now." He just candidly said what many people think. It takes courage to follow the suffering servant.

It does not take that much courage to write a book about the Kingdom. We did not want to write about the Kingdom until we were seriously engaged in living new things we began learning two years ago. As we have sought to practice kingdom principles along with other disciples, we have confirmed that living these principles is much harder than writing about them. So are we writing now because we have "arrived"? Not by a long shot. We would quickly say with Paul:

> Not that I have already attained this—that is, I have
> not already been perfected—but I strive to lay hold
> of that for which Christ Jesus also laid hold of me.
> (Philippians 3:12 NET)

If anything, in our minds, we are further off than when we started; our knowledge keeps outrunning our actions, and so we—like everyone else—need much grace to live up to what we have been called to. But, thanks be to God that grace is at the heart of the kingdom message. Thanks be to God that his grace is sufficient (2 Corinthians 12:9).

We really cannot think of anything we want more than to see the Kingdom being lived out by today's church. We pray as did our brothers and sisters in Acts 4 for the courage to speak the message anywhere, and for the credibility of our message to be strengthened by the integrity of our lives.

△

For a moment we want to address some different types of people that we believe may be readers of this book.

First, there are some of you who consider yourselves long-time believers. You "received" Christ in some form at some point in the past. You have had a Christian identity for many years. Church life is part of who you are, but there is certainly nothing subversive or threatening about the nature of your spiritual life. You blend in quite well with everyone at the office and in the neighborhood. You don't have much feeling of being an alien or stranger in this world. You make decisions pretty much the way everyone else does, and you seldom ask yourself "What does seeking first the Kingdom mean in this situation?" You can't think of a time when you have read Jesus' teachings and wrestled in prayer about how to obey them.

Given the dramatic nature of the age-to-come life and the way it challenges the present age, can you feel good about staying where you are? Can you see that life in the Kingdom of God will never be a "normal" life by the world's standards? Do you dare go for something more? Do you hear Jesus calling you to change?

There are others of you who made a serious commitment to Jesus as adults or mature young people. You counted the cost (Luke 14), and after doing that you wanted to be his disciple. You gave up an old way of life. You made some radical decisions. You had a kingdom heart. It showed up in your actions. You experienced opposition and suffered persecution. You saw some great things. But the churches you were in made mistakes. People were hurt. Your faith was hurt. You made it through and didn't leave, but it affected you. Now you are still seeking Jesus, or at least holding on to him. However, if we drew the continuum below, at which number would you see yourself?

Cautious Christian ---------------------- Radical Disciple
   1   2   3   4   5   6   7   8   9   10

Are you in awe of God's Kingdom? Does it excite you? Are you still prayerfully receiving it? Do you have a sense of wonder about how much of it can still come to your life? Are you open to new things and eager to obey even if that means big trouble?

Would you say you tend to be more toward the cautious side than the radical side? We suspect that many of us have allowed time and life and pain to erode our convictions and drain out of us a pure kingdom heart. But, since the future has broken into the present and the Kingdom of God is among us, our hearts can be revived. If we are just not sure we want to step out again, Jesus assures us, "Do not be afraid, little flock, for your Father has been pleased to give you the kingdom" (Luke 12:32).

And finally, we say a word to leaders. Maybe you are in one of the two groups already addressed, but we end with a special word to you. Examine your convictions. Evaluate your teaching. Is your main message the same as Jesus' main message? Are you calling people to live the age-to-come life? Are you teaching others to teach the age-to-come life? Are you committed to teaching those who follow your leadership to obey, by the grace of God and the power of the Holy Spirit, the Sermon on the Mount? Do you want to obey it more than you want to explain it away? Are you getting input from others to help you live it? What is something new you have learned about kingdom living in the last year? How are you trying to put it into practice? Are you growing and changing still?

If you are a leader, you are influencing people. They know you either as a religious person or a kingdom person. They know you as a prideful person or a humble person. As a self-absorbed person or a caring person. And you affect their lives. You help them see the Kingdom or you block their view. So we urge you, face the challenge of leading others in the kingdom life. Let it humble you, so you lead with poverty of Spirit and meekness. But rely on God's Spirit so you will lead with courage.

(If you don't fit into any of these categories, we pray that you will find the Jesus we have talked about to be a compelling figure you will want to know much more about.)

△

The Kingdom came in Jesus, and waves of it are still coming. The church today can live the kingdom life. It will take awe, openness, much prayer, fellowship and obedience; it will produce confidence and courage to speak. But "Jesus Christ is the same yesterday, today and forever" (Hebrews 13:8). The king is still the king and his Kingdom is still the Kingdom.

In his book *Resident Aliens*, Stanley Hauweras has a chapter called "Salvation As Adventure." He ends it with these words:

> When we are baptized, we (like the first disciples) jump on a moving train. As disciples, we do not so much accept a creed, or come to a clear sense of self-understanding… we become part of a journey that began long before we got here and shall continue long after we are gone.[3]

The kingdom adventure train is rolling. We are called to jump on board. We do not know where it will take us, how many ups and downs there will be, how wild the ride will get, how subversive it will seem to some, or how many "normal cultural Christian reflexes" we will have to give up. We will expect it to be challenging, but in the final analysis, we won't care as long as it leads toward God, helps us live like Jesus, and helps the Kingdom be the Light to the Nations!

Questions for Study and Discussion

1. In the church where you are a member, are there any matters that need to be addressed so the church can be seen as a place where Isaiah 11 is being shown to the world?

2. How do you see disciples being aliens and strangers in the world, and what effect does that have on them? What must Christian relationships and Christian fellowship be like in order to strengthen us in an environment that may be hostile?

3. What have you learned about living the kingdom life from other disciples? How would you assess your own attitude about learning a lot more?

4. Why is it incomprehensible that a kingdom person would not be telling others about what he or she has found?

5. As you prepare to tell others the good news of the Kingdom, what is the most encouraging word you find in this last charge Jesus gives in Matthew 28?

6. Why does it take courage to live the kingdom life, and where do you find the courage to live it?

7. Where did you put yourself on the continuum between Cautious Christian and Radical Disciple? How do you feel about where you are, and what input do you want from others?

8. If you are a leader in any area, are there ways you have not modeled the kingdom life?

9. Is salvation an adventure for you? Did you jump on a moving train? How important is it to you to know exactly where it is going?

10. Make a clear statement about how you feel about Jesus and the Kingdom.

NOTE: We include discussion questions at the end of each chapter, but they are also available on the web with permission to print and copy. (kingdombooks-vol1.blogspot.com)

6

The Kingdom Is Not Yet

THE NEW HEAVEN AND NEW EARTH

First, there is an Old Testament vision of a coming Kingdom. Then, in Jesus we have the announcement that the long wait is over and that the Kingdom has come. In his life and work, his word and deeds we see it breaking into this age. We see the Kingdom bring into existence the church so that the good news can be lived out and taken to all nations. We see what the church must be to fulfill that role. But finally, we see that while the Kingdom is here and now, the Kingdom is also *not yet*.

Kingdom citizens have tasted the powers of the coming age (Hebrews 6:5), but have not fully entered the coming age. They have received back a hundred fold anything they have given up in the present age, but in the coming age they will receive eternal life (Mark 10:30). Jesus has won the victory through the cross and the resurrection, but as Hebrews puts it, "Yet, at present we do not see everything subject to him"

(Hebrews 2:8). In Jesus, the gospel, and the new community of faith, we see amazing things, especially lives that are changed, but the fullness of the age to come is "not yet."

Just as surely as the words of the prophets were fulfilled in the coming of Jesus, the words of Jesus himself will be fulfilled. He will return and bring all the fullness, all the wonder and all the glory of his Kingdom, his reign and his rule. And then it will be said, "The kingdom of this world has become the kingdom of our Lord and of his Christ, and he will reign forever and ever" (Revelation 11:15).

But we live between the times. We live between (1) his first coming with the appearance of the Kingdom among us, and (2) his glorious return. So we wait. Paul, in several places describes our watchful waiting:

- We wait eagerly for our adoption as sons, the redemption of our bodies (Romans 8:19).
- We eagerly wait for our Lord Jesus Christ to be revealed (1 Corinthians 1:7).
- We wait for [God's] Son from heaven, whom he raised from the dead—Jesus who rescues from the coming wrath (1 Thessalonians 1:10).
- We wait for the blessed hope—the glorious appearing of our great God and Savior, Jesus Christ (Titus 2:13).

What we seek to do in this chapter is to answer two questions: (1) What can we know about the new world we are waiting for? and (2) What should we do while we wait?

What Can We Know?

When all we have ever known is life in this present age, it is naturally difficult to imagine what life will be like in another. We are confident that for God's people it will be a better place, but we are also given some truths in Scripture that can add substance to our expectations as well as correct some common misconceptions. There are five passages of Scripture that serve as the logical place to begin:

1. Isaiah 65:17
   Behold, I will create new heavens
        and a new earth.
   The former things will not be remembered,
        nor will they come to mind.

2. Isaiah 66:22
   "As the new heavens and the new earth that I make will endure before me," declares the LORD, "so will your name and descendants endure."

3. 2 Peter 3:13
   But in keeping with his promise we are looking forward to a new heaven and a new earth, the home of righteousness.

4. Revelation 21:1
   Then I saw a new heaven and a new earth, for the first heaven and the first earth had passed away, and there was no longer any sea.

5. Romans 8:18–23
   I consider that our present sufferings are not worth comparing with the glory that will be revealed in us.

> The creation waits in eager expectation for the sons
> of God to be revealed. For the creation was sub-
> jected to frustration, not by its own choice, but by
> the will of the one who subjected it, in hope that
> the creation itself will be liberated from its bondage
> to decay and brought into the glorious freedom of
> the children of God.
>
> We know that the whole creation has been
> groaning as in the pains of childbirth right up to
> the present time. Not only so, but we ourselves,
> who have the firstfruits of the Spirit, groan inwardly
> as we wait eagerly for our adoption as sons, the
> redemption of our bodies.

It is clear from these texts that our future, after the
resurrection, will be where there is a new heaven (or
heavens) and a new earth. Remarkably, until recently, little
has been said or written about this subject. Isaiah, whose
work has been such a key in this study of the Kingdom,
once again stands out, telling us that there will be a new
earth.[1]

Then in a great chapter on life in the Spirit, Paul tells
us that not only is man groaning for redemption, but the
physical creation does as well. Obviously, he is referring
to all of creation—the universe, the earth, animal and plant
life. His words seem to assume that creation's yearning will
be satisfied, and that it too will be brought into the glorious
freedom of the children of God.

Surveys have shown that most people think of heaven
as a "place" that is spiritual and not physical, whatever
that means. They usually think it will be inhabited by

disembodied spirits. But then because they have never known anything but a physical world and cannot envision disembodied spirits, the whole idea seems vague. As we have pointed out, most people think they are going there, but understandably, they hold that belief with little excitement or enthusiasm.

Scripture never taught us to think like this. These ideas come from Greek philosophy, particularly from Platonism—where the body is viewed as the prison house of the soul and where one looks forward to the soul eventually escaping into the great "oversoul."[2] In Platonism there is nothing good about physicality—it only deceives and hides from us the true realities. Unfortunately this entirely anti-biblical view made its way into Christendom and still influences much thinking about spirituality and the new world Jesus will bring.

Paul says that our present sufferings are not worth comparing to the glory that will be revealed in us, but he does not say, "You cannot relate the new world to our present world, because the two have no continuity." No, that is not his message! He speaks of the redemption of our bodies. The new world will be fashioned on what we already know something about—but in a redeemed form. We will have bodies; they will just be redeemed and more glorious bodies (Philippians 3:21). This has descriptive meaning for us as physical beings. And parallel to this, there will be the creation, and we know something about it. In the new world you will find the creation, except it will be a redeemed and even more glorious creation. And that has meaning for us.

Let's think about the human body, which in its present form is already remarkable. In each of your body's cells is a DNA molecule containing detailed information, but it is so thin and coiled that if you could uncoil it and stretch it out, it would be more than two miles long. The total length of DNA in one adult human being is estimated to be seventy times the round-trip distance from the earth to the sun.

The list of amazing facts about our bodies is almost endless: It is estimated that in the average human brain there are 100 million firing neurons and perhaps a 100 *trillion* synapses (a structure that serves as a connecting point with another cell). Our lungs contain over 300,000 capillaries. Each kidney contains one million individual glomeruli (filters) and one million nephrons (distributors), and each kidney processes more that 200 quarts of blood a day. The system of blood vessels in the whole body—arteries, veins and capillaries—is over 60,000 miles long. The adult heart pumps about five quarts of blood each minute and approximately 2,000 gallons of blood daily throughout the body, with the heart beating about 100,000 times each day. On the one hand, we are "fearfully and wonderfully made" (Psalm 139:14), but on the other hand, Paul says Jesus "will transform our lowly bodies so they will be like this glorious body" (Philippians 3:21). Can you imagine?

These already astonishing bodies, which, of course, still do break down, thus are "lowly." But these bodies will be redeemed and become something more glorious (and the two of us guys with MS are really excited about this!).

In the same way we can look at our planet and think about what it may be like to have a new and redeemed earth. Our present earth has a remarkable atmosphere, hydrosphere, geo-sphere and biosphere. Pictures from the Apollo space missions showed us its incredible beauty, unlike that of any celestial body ever seen in our universe. Yes, we have hurricanes, tor-nadoes, floods and earthquakes, so it is not perfect (remember Paul does say it is groaning for redemption). But the combina-tion of temperature, atmosphere, light and gravity makes the earth an inhabitable, often flourishing, frequently spectacular and completely unique place as far as anyone knows.

But in the age to come there will be a new earth. Some-thing already quite astonishing will receive the ultimate up-grade. All the upsides will be magnified. All the downsides will be gone. Can you imagine?

The futuristic blockbuster *Avatar* captivated people's imagination with its surreal beauty, florescent plants and spectacular floating mountains—all seen in vivid 3D—on the planet Pandora. So mesmerized by and fixated on the glories of this fictional place, some are reportedly no longer interested in living "the gray humdrum life on planet Earth." Supposedly there is a new type of depression in the wake of the movie. It is known as the Pandora Effect and occurs in people who realize that they will never really experience the life they saw on Pandora. But just imagine: If the human mind and a little Hollywood wizardry can create such inspiring beauty, what will be true of the new earth produced by God the Creator?

Having said this, we have only considered the physicality of the new age. Think next of the musical, literary and artistic gifts given to man. If a deaf Beethoven could write "The Moonlight Sonata" and "The Third Piano Concerto," what will redeemed man be able to do? Mozart began composing at age five and was composing operas at fourteen; by age fifteen he had composed twenty-three symphonies; and by the end of his life at age thirty-five he had composed forty-one symphonies; fifty-one concertos for piano, violin, bassoon, horn, trumpet and woodwinds; plus numerous operas, serenades, marches and dances.

Can we imagine what the arts will be like within an assembly of redeemed people? A very conservative estimate is that more than two million songs have been recorded in the United States and the United Kingdom since the recording industry began a hundred years or so ago. Can we imagine what will happen in the coming age?

Music is an astonishing gift from God. We hope someday to see a paper written on the "Musical Argument for the Existence of God." It would likely be more compelling than the ontological argument and more fun than the cosmological argument!

In a scholarly article titled "The Nature of Music from a Biological Perspective," Isabelle Peretz of the University of Montreal says this:

Music has emerged spontaneously and in parallel in all known human societies. Although we do not know when music emerged because there are no fossil records of singing, archeological evidence shows a continuous record of musical instruments, dating back to at least 30,000 years (D'Errico et al., 2003). Thus, music is an ancient capacity rather than the recent creation of a single intelligence. Music appears to transcend time, place, and culture…. Everyone from all walks of life and all cultures is musical to some extent. Unless they are tone-deaf, all humans exhibit a precocious inclination for music. In short, music appears as natural as language is.[3]

As her paper shows, music is as fascinating and complex as it is often beautiful, moving, inspiring or soothing. Given the incredible variety of music in our present age, what will it be like in the coming age?

And then there are so many other arts, writing skills and astonishing intellectual gifts that we do not have time to speak of. We have every reason to believe that all of these will continue but be magnified many times in the coming age.

But last, we come to the greatest occurrence of all in the new age. Already in this present age, disciples of Jesus have "every spiritual blessing in Christ" (Ephesians 1:3), but in the new age we will realize these blessings in total clarity, no longer seeing them as a poor reflection as in a mirror. Then we shall see face to face. Now we know in part; then we shall know fully, even as we will be fully known (1 Corinthians 13:12). There our eyes will be fully opened, and we will grasp with all the people of the Kingdom, how high and long and deep and wide is the love of Christ, and it will no longer surpass our knowledge (Ephesians 3:16–19). We will experience it and we will fully grasp it and understand it. Can you imagine?

The chapter on heaven in *Worship the King* by Henry Kriete may be one of the most inspiring you will ever read on this subject. In one place he writes:

> ...words like "glory," "all," "life," "seed," "power"—not to mention "God"—all the words the Bible uses to describe heaven—are pregnant with meaning. Each contains a concept that is real, but ungraspable. These words provide us a taste. They are but hints and shadows. Through them we have a veiled sense of heaven..."[4]

Several pages later he continues:

> In heaven, Paul says, we shall be "swallowed up in life" (2 Corinthians 5:4). That even sounds good, doesn't it? Inhaled, swallowed, enveloped and invaded by life itself, life that springs from the source of all life, from the architect of living things, from the eternal life himself.
>
> We will inherit from God—catch your breath—all things (Romans 8:32). Everything that God's mind can imagine, that his power can accomplish, that his love can lavish, shall be given to us. We are his offspring, true sons and daughters with the legal rights of heirs. We own "the whole estate" (Galatians 4:1). We have the right to eat in the paradise of God (Revelation 2:7). When the Bible says "all things," it means "all things." And why should it not? As we have said previously, if God "did not spare his own Son but gave him up for us all—how will he

not also, along with him, graciously give us all things? (Romans 8:32).[5]

In the new heaven and new earth we will be overwhelmed with goodness, saturated with kindness, and overflowing with joy. The fruit of the Spirit will be ours in abundance. The relationships those qualities will produce will be indescribable; only there we *will have* more than enough words to describe them.

But where will all this happen? In the new heaven? In the new earth? Or in both places? As N.T. Wright shows so well, heaven and earth are both real places, with important differences and an important relationship. Here is his helpful description:

> ...when the Bible speaks of heaven and earth, it is not talking about two localities related to each other within the same space time continuum or about a non-physical world in contrast to a physical one but about two different *kinds* of what we call space and different kinds of what we call matter...and quite possibly what we call time.[6]

Wright praises C.S. Lewis as one who helps us in *The Chronicles of Narnia* to see how two different worlds can relate and overlap. Of course, such an idea has become quite popular in contemporary fiction, television and cinema.

In this context, Wright calls our attention to the importance of something we often give scant attention to: the Ascension of Jesus, recorded both at the end of Luke and the beginning of Acts. In this event, we have the fully divine and fully human Jesus passing as a resurrected embodied human (in Wright's words, "a more solidly embodied human than we are") from one space or realm to another. He leaves earth and ascends to heaven. He is absent from earth but present in heaven. This shows, Wright says, "…that God's space and ours—heaven and earth, in other words—are, though very different, not far from each other."[7]

That is an insight to ponder, but even if they were far from each other, it would not matter, (1) because God's power can traverse any gulf, and (2) because when he comes back, it is not to take us "up" to a distant and strange heaven, but it is to bring himself and his heaven *down to live with us* in the new earth. Listen to the words of Revelation 21:

> Then I saw a new heaven and a new earth, for the first heaven and the first earth had passed away, and there was no longer any sea. I saw the Holy City, the new Jerusalem, coming down out of heaven from God, prepared as a bride beautifully dressed for her husband. And I heard a loud voice from the throne saying, "Now the dwelling of God is with men, and he will live with them. They will be his people, and God himself will be with them and be their God. He will wipe every tear from their eyes. There will be no more death or mourning or crying or pain, for the old order of things has passed away." (vv1–4)

When Jesus returns, bringing with him the new Jerusalem, these two realms, that can and do overlap now, will become *one and the same space and matter* in the consummation of the Kingdom.[8] In the words of the beautiful hymn, "This Is My Father's World":

> This is my Father's world.
> O let me ne'er forget
> That though the wrong seems oft so strong,
> God is the ruler yet.
> This is my Father's world,
> The battle is not done:
> Jesus who died shall be satisfied,
> *And earth and Heav'n be one.* (emphasis added)

It is fascinating to think about the marriage of heaven and earth, but the more important thing is what this says about God. To the very end, the God who humbled himself and took the form of a servant will be stunning us with his humility and his kindness. He does not say, "Come up here and live with me in my heaven, but he comes down to us—*again*—bringing heaven with him, so he can live with us on our earth—a new earth he creates for us. He does it all for us so we can have the joy of being his people and having him be our God. *The new heaven will be the new earth. The new earth will be the new heaven.* So, all who want heaven on earth desire a reality not a fantasy. To use our best scholarly word: Wow!

No wonder Peter wrote to his people: "Therefore, prepare your minds for action; be self-controlled; set your hope fully on the grace to be given you when Jesus Christ is revealed" (1 Peter 1:13). Peter believes it makes a difference in our lives now, as we live in the overlap of earth and heaven, as we live for a while as strangers and aliens, to set our hope on this flood of extravagant generosity coming our way. It will awe us, comfort us and inspire us, and remind us that we indeed have found life to the full.

How Do We Wait?

From the passages we cited at the beginning of this chapter and many others like them, we can see that part of life in the Kingdom is waiting, and yet waiting eagerly. There is certainly nothing wrong with eagerly desiring the new age that God will give us, but it is not only *eager* waiting but *faithful* waiting that God looks for. But how do we do that?

We aren't sure how it is in some of the world, but we know that Americans hate to wait. An AP poll found that the two places we hate to wait the most are the grocery store and the department of motor vehicles. Sixty percent of those polled said they can wait in line no more than fifteen minutes before losing their cool. Eighty percent said their patience runs out if they are on hold on a phone call for more than five minutes. It doesn't get better as we age. The survey found older people to be more impatient than younger ones.

Between the two of us we have spent our share of time waiting in doctor's offices. We have learned that it is a good idea to take a book, a computer or something to work on, so that we make the most of the time while we wait. This is what we are considering in this section—how to make the most of the time while we wait.

First, let's notice how not to wait.

In the first century, as in later centuries, there were those who thought the final in-breaking of the age to come was going to happen right away. In fact, that was most certainly the dominant thinking among early Christians. Given the admonitions that Paul speaks to the Thessalonians, it seems there were some who expected an imminent return of Jesus and no longer saw the need to keep a job. Their idea of waiting was, well, just waiting. So Paul writes:

> For even when we were with you, we gave you this rule: "If a man will not work, he shall not eat."
> We hear that some among you are idle. They are not busy; they are busybodies. Such people we command and urge in the Lord Jesus Christ to settle down and earn the bread they eat. And as for you, brothers, never tire of doing what is right. (2 Thessalonians 3:10–13)

There is a kind of false spirituality (something akin to ancient Gnosticism) that reasons like this: What happens in this world is really unimportant, and we just need to keep our eyes on what is coming from the next. This is some people's idea of "fixing your mind on things above." But what happens in this world does matter, and we need to be "redeeming the time" (Colossians 4:5 ASV). Part of faithful kingdom living, of course, is providing for ourselves and our families (2 Thessalonians 3:10, 1 Timothy 5:8). Who listens to a message about a changed life from those who are lazy and irresponsible?

I (Tom) spent a good bit of time with my grandfather at his place in the tiny burgh of Waterloo, Alabama. He was an extremely hard-working man with rough callused hands. The amount of hours he spent in grueling field work under the Alabama summer sun is beyond my comprehension. However, when we came to see him and my grandmother, we would drive up and find them sitting on the front porch of their tin-roofed house with its faux-brick siding, going easily back and forth in the big porch swing like they didn't have a thing to do. That sure made going for a visit with them seem like "summer time and the living is easy," but it belied what hard workers they both were.

When I consider this memory, the kind of waiting the New Testament pictures is better symbolized by what my grandfather was doing well before our arrival. Looking forward to moving on to when the "mortal will put on immortality," Paul writes this to the Corinthian disciples:

> Therefore, my dear brothers, stand firm. Let nothing move you. Always give yourselves fully to the work of the Lord, because you know that your labor in the Lord is not in vain. (1 Corinthians 15:58)

This is not sitting-by-the-phone-and-listening-for-a-call waiting. It is not swinging-on-the-porch waiting. It is active waiting. It is working while you wait.

But lest we encourage a kingdom lifestyle that leads to a string of burnouts, there is something to be said for the rhythm of life I saw in my grandparents. They knew how to work, but they also knew how to turn the motors off for a while and just sit and relax. The tenor of life for kingdom people will be one of giving themselves fully to the work of the Lord, but they will also need to remember that the Sabbath day of rest was his idea and find ways to practice that principle in the new-covenant Kingdom.

Second, we must wait trusting God's means and God's timing.

Trying to make something happen on our timetable or as we think it ought to be is not the kingdom way. That is true if we are talking about the final consummation of all things or the next phase of our lives right here.

I (Steve) was reading through the middle chapters in Isaiah as we were finishing this book, and these words struck me: "For the Lord is a faithful God. Blessed are those who wait for his help" (Isaiah 30:18 NLT). In the context, God is concerned about his people who were making alliances with other nations to protect them from their enemies instead of relying on him, trusting him.

At this writing, Diane and I are in the middle of a move, after being in Nashville for eight years—about as long as we have ever lived anywhere—and the passage seemed especially appropriate. They say moving is one of life's most stressful events, which includes all of this and more: putting a house on the market, painting it to make it look better, making decisions about the color of paint, and pondering "Do we take this, give it away or toss it?"

Then there are going-away parties and last chance opportunities to get with folks before we leave. It is so easy for me not to trust, not to pray, and to just have a "get 'er done" attitude, forgetting all about the king in his Kingdom—the one who is really in charge of all of this. After all, it was his idea that we make this move right now—certainly not mine.

So whatever problems you are facing—the challenges of moving, the difficulty of looking for a job, the fear of inoperable cancer, the painstaking recovery after a flood, or the struggle with chronic pain (most of us know people in all of these situations right now)—the real challenge is to wait on the Lord. Don't run ahead; don't try to manipulate things, and don't compromise kingdom integrity, "for the Lord is a faithful God and blessed are those who wait."

This is true also as we look forward to a whole new and better world where none of these other problems will exist. He will bless us as we wait faithfully.

Finally, we wait, in one sense, by not waiting.

We wait by not waiting until we are in heaven to put into practice God's will as it is in heaven. That has been perhaps the main theme of this book and a right place for us to end. In Jesus and the Kingdom, the new age has overlapped the present age, and we who follow him are squarely in that overlap. Our bodies are in this age, but our ears are listening to instructions from the next. *We wait by fixing our minds*

*on things above and then living right now by that wisdom
coming down from above.*

God may delay the final coming of the new age, for one
reason, to give more people time to repent (2 Peter 3:8–9).
But whatever his reason, kingdom people are to be using
the time to get the message to others primarily by living "on
earth as it is in heaven." We wait by practicing all those principles we talked about in the last two chapters—showing
ourselves to be an outpost of heaven in this world.

But as we work hard, we must do it, to borrow from a
Eugene Peterson title, with "a long obedience in the same
direction."[9] Hebrews 11 describes Old Testament heroes
who commended themselves through faithful waiting. The
writer describes them this way:

> All these people were still living by faith when they
> died. They did not receive the things promised;
> they only saw them and welcomed them from a
> distance. And they admitted that they were aliens
> and strangers on earth.
>
> People who say such things show that they
> are looking for a country of their own. If they had
> been thinking of the country they had left, they
> would have had opportunity to return. Instead,
> they were longing for a better country—a heavenly
> one. Therefore God is not ashamed to be called
> their God, for he has prepared a city for them.
> (vv13–16)

There is the greatest connection with what we do with
the *now* and what is *yet to come.* Faithful waiting involves

trusting even when what we wait for is only seen dimly in the distance or maybe not seen at all. Biblical history teaches us that God is in no hurry. He is concerned not with speed but with obedience, not with quickness but character.

The church today could certainly use a greater sense of expectation about the return of Jesus, but what we may need more is an expectation of how God can work through our faithfulness now while we wait. From the amount of material we find in Scripture, it is obvious God does not intend that we be preoccupied with the details of the age to come. Rather, his concern is that we know and do his will in the present age.

△

And so we conclude by letting the Bible tell its own story and give its own call. Listen carefully (emphasis added):

> "The time has come," he said. "*The kingdom of God* is near. Repent and believe the good news!"[10]... "Do not be afraid, little flock, for your Father has been pleased to give you the kingdom"[11]... "The kingdom of heaven is like treasure hidden in a field. When a man found it, he hid it again, and then in his joy went and sold all he had and bought that field."[12]

> "But seek first his kingdom and his righteousness, and all these things will be given to you as well"[13]... Peter said to him, "We have left everything to follow you!" "I tell you the truth," Jesus replied, "no one who has left home or brothers or sisters or mother or father or children or fields for me and the

gospel will fail to receive a hundred times as much in this present age (homes, brothers, sisters, mothers, children and fields—and with them, persecutions) and in the age to come, eternal life. But many who are first will be last, and the last first." [14]

To this you were called, because Christ suffered for you, leaving you an example, that you should follow in his steps. "He committed no sin, and no deceit was found in his mouth." When they hurled their insults at him, he did not retaliate; when he suffered, he made no threats. Instead, he entrusted himself to him who judges justly. He himself bore our sins in his body on the tree, so that we might die to sins and live for righteousness; by his wounds you have been healed. [15]

...and this water symbolizes baptism that now saves you also—not the removal of dirt from the body but the pledge of a good conscience toward God. It saves you by the resurrection of Jesus Christ, who has gone into heaven and is at God's right hand—with angels, authorities and powers in submission to him. [16]

Now that you have purified yourselves by obeying the truth so that you have sincere love for your brothers, love one another deeply, from the heart. For you have been born again, not of perishable seed, but of imperishable, through the living and enduring word of God. [17] ... But you are a chosen people, a royal priesthood, a holy nation, a people belonging to God, that you may declare the praises of him who called you out of darkness into his wonderful light. Once you were not a people, but now you are the people of God; once you had not received mercy, but now you have received mercy. Dear friends, I urge you, as aliens and strangers in the world, to abstain from sinful desires, which war against your soul. Live such good lives among the pagans that, though they accuse you of doing wrong, they may see your good deeds and glorify God on the day he visits us.[18]...

[It is you who] ...have been enlightened, who have tasted the heavenly gift, who have shared in the Holy Spirit, who have tasted the goodness of the word of God and the powers of the coming age[19]... Therefore set your hope fully on the grace to be given you when Jesus Christ is revealed[20] ... Since everything will be destroyed in this way, what kind of people ought you to be? You ought to live holy and godly lives as you look forward to the day of God and speed its coming...[21] Therefore, since we are receiving a kingdom that cannot be shaken, let us be thankful, and so worship God acceptably with reverence and awe, for our "God is a consuming fire."[22]

Then I saw a new heaven and a new earth, for the first heaven and the first earth had passed away, and there was no longer any sea. I saw the Holy City, the new Jerusalem, coming down out of heaven from God, prepared as a bride beautifully dressed for her husband. And I heard a loud voice from the throne saying, "Now the dwelling of God is with men, and he will live with them. They will be his people, and God himself will be with them and be their God. He will wipe every tear from their eyes. There will be no more death or mourning or crying or pain, for the old order of things has passed away."[23]

...some things are worth waiting for...and living for... and dying for. Our Father, may your kingdom come!

Questions for Study and Discussion

1. Describe what feelings and thoughts this chapter brought up for you?

2. What has been your view of heaven, and how could these thoughts change the way you see it?

3. The authors had questions about including this chapter because they know readers could get concerned about the details of the coming age and let the novelty of this cause them to forget the rest of the book. In your case, is there any reason for concern here?

4. If you are discussing these questions in a group, let each person share the most beautiful place they have ever been on earth and what it was about the place that touched them. As you do this, keep thinking about the new earth.

5. How can the realities of the coming age be an inspiration and a help to us in living heaven's way right now in the present age?

6. What would be some wrong ways for a kingdom person to let thoughts of the age to come influence his or her life?

7. How do you want to show the world around you that you trust God's timing and God's means?
8. What are three decisions you have made or will make because of this study of the Kingdom?

NOTE: We include discussion questions at the end of each chapter, but they are also available on the web with permission to print and copy. (kingdombooks-vol1.blogspot.com)

Appendix 1

The Kingdom and the Church

THE ISSUE OF CHRONOLOGY

The contention that the church that began on the Day of Pentecost is interchangeable with the idea of the Kingdom runs into severe problems when passages such as these found below are considered. They all show that the Kingdom was coming in the life and ministry of Jesus and that when Jesus preached the good news of the Kingdom it was because people could respond and receive it through his ministry. The coming of the Spirit on Pentecost was a most significant event, but the Kingdom had already been breaking in as we see in these verses where emphasis has been added.

Matthew 4:23
Jesus went throughout Galilee, teaching in their synagogues, preaching the good news of the kingdom, and healing every disease and sickness among the people.

The good news of the kingdom was that God was breaking in to rescue his people as evidenced by the works of healing. This was good news right then and there. It was not just good news that they could become part of the church in two or three years.

Matthew 5:3
"Blessed are the poor in spirit, for theirs *is* the kingdom of heaven."

Matthew 5:10
"Blessed are those who are persecuted because of righteousness, for theirs *is* the kingdom of heaven."

In these "bookends" for the Beatitudes Jesus was giving people a message to put into practice and realize the fulfillment of the Kingdom in their day. With attitudes and action they experienced the reign of God. Notice "theirs *is*" the kingdom, not "theirs *will be...*"

Matthew 21:31b–32
Jesus said to them, "I tell you the truth, the tax collectors and the *prostitutes are entering* the kingdom of God ahead of you. For John came to you to show you the way of righteousness, and you did not believe him, but the tax collectors and the prostitutes did. And even after you saw this, you did not repent and believe him."

The *prima facie* meaning is that disreputables of society "*are* entering the kingdom of God" because they believed the preaching of John and responded in repentance (and, of course, in the baptism he always administered). Not only were people entering the Kingdom before Pentecost; they were entering it before Jesus even fully began his ministry or at least before John's death.

Matthew 23:13

"Woe to you, teachers of the law and Pharisees, you hypocrites! You shut the kingdom of heaven in men's faces. You yourselves *do not enter*, nor will you let those enter who are trying to."

In Jesus' own life before his death and resurrection and before the Spirit was sent on Pentecost, the Pharisees were not entering the kingdom, but by their lives they were shutting the kingdom of heaven in men's faces. They weren't entering, *though they could have entered then*. So in Matthew 21 and Matthew 23, we have the starkest of contrasts: The prostitutes and tax collectors *were entering* the Kingdom during the life of Jesus, but the Pharisees were keeping themselves and others out. If we try substituting the word "church" for "Kingdom" in these texts, we end up with something that clearly does not work. At this point no one was entering the church.

Luke 11:19–20

"Now if I drive out demons by Beelzebub, by whom do your followers drive them out? So then, they will be your judges. But if I drive out demons by the finger of God, then *the kingdom of God has come to you.*" (NASB—has "come upon you")

Though the Pharisees argued that Jesus drove out demons by Satan's power, seemingly no one doubted that they were driven out. Jesus' point is that this is evidence that *the kingdom had come* upon them right then and there.

Luke 17:20–21

Now having been questioned by the Pharisees as to when the kingdom of God was coming, He answered them and said, "The kingdom of God is not coming with signs to be observed; nor will they say, `Look, here it is!' or, 'There it is!' For behold, *the kingdom of God is in your midst.*" (NASB)

Whether this rendering is used or the more questionable "the kingdom of God is within you," Jesus is still speaking in the present tense. The kingdom was there right then in the ministry of Jesus.

Matthew 11:12

"From the days of John the Baptist until now, the kingdom of heaven *has been* forcefully advancing, and forceful men lay hold of it."

While interpreters differ on the meaning of the last part of this passage, there can be no question about the portion that says "From the days of John until now, the kingdom of heaven has been forcefully advancing…" As has been shown throughout this book, the Kingdom was coming in all kinds of ways and waves in Jesus' ministry, and here even since the days of John, who was long dead before the events of Pentecost.

Appendix 2
Life in the Spirit Version 2.0

It may be helpful to think of life in the Spirit in three versions. Version 1.0 is here in the present age. We live as those who have already tasted the power of the coming age. The Spirit is at work in our lives guaranteeing what is to come. Life has problems, and we still feel the "fallen" nature of our world, but we have experienced that the Lord is good, and we find great meaning in walking with him. In Version 1.0 we have found "life to the full." Eternal life has begun here (John 17:3).

Version 3.0 is what we discussed in chapter 6—what it will be like when the Kingdom comes in all its fullness and when there will be no more "not yet." In between will be Version 2.0. This is what we will experience after our death, but before the Second Coming, the general resurrection of the dead, and the judgment. We are probably more accurate not to call this "heaven," and at brother Faithful Disciple's funeral, it is probably not best to say he has died and gone to heaven unless you mean something other than the final heaven. (But we also aren't suggesting you say he now has Life in the Spirit 2.0!)

We aren't given a lot of detail about 3.0. We are given even less about 2.0. We know that Version 1.0 Life in the Spirit is very good. And we do know that Version 2.0 is going to "be better by far" (thank you, Paul, for that word in Philippians 1:23). Finally, we know that version 3.0 is going to be off the charts.

For those who have fears that Version 2.0 may be a long dreary wait as a disembodied spirit, let us assure you that when God does an upgrade, it will never seem like a downgrade (and for the computer-savvy among us: There will be no compatibility issues—none!). Whatever God has in mind for that intermediate state, which likely is what the New Testament calls "paradise" (Luke 23:43, 2 Corinthians 12:4, Revelation 2:7), it will be "far better." Having begun life in the Spirit and having enjoyed the love of God in this world, those who are faithful will never find it interrupted (Romans 8:38–39). And Paul seems to assure us that in version 2.0 we will have some kind of good body (heavenly dwelling), though it will not yet be the glorious body we will have at the resurrection when Jesus returns (compare 2 Corinthians 5:4–5 and Philippians 3:20–21).

Those who want to pursue these matters will likely benefit from an excellent CD series by Douglas Jacoby titled *What Happens after We Die?* (Spring, TX: IPI).

NOTES

Introduction

1. This count of one hundred includes all the references to "the kingdom of heaven" that are found in Matthew. Though Matthew will use the term "kingdom of God," he prefers "kingdom of heaven." It is usually thought that this is due to the fact that Matthew's Gospel seems to be written to a largely Jewish audience, who were not comfortable using the name of God because of its sacredness. A word such as "heaven" would often be used to represent God. However, there are others who have challenged this assumption, while not offering any suggestion as to why Matthew chooses that wording.

2. Some may feel that this puts too much blame on Constantine and not enough on the leaders of the church, who, after all, did not have to cooperate with the changes that Constantine wanted to make. It does appear that a church weary with persecution and basking in the favor of an emperor for a change, found the temptations of an easier way to practice their faith so tempting that they began a slow drift into being a state church profoundly influenced by the wisdom of worldly sources.

3. Lee Camp uses this language and suggests that many of these "Christian reflexes" may have more to do with paganism

than with early Christianity. Lee Camp, *Mere Discipleship: Radical Christianity in a Rebellious World* (Grand Rapids: Brazos/Baker, 2003), 53.

4. Some years ago I (Tom) described the grace of God as the trunk of the Christian tree from which all else grows. Thomas Jones, *Strong in the Grace* (Spring Hill, TN: DPI, 2004). This present book does not represent a departure from the thinking about grace expressed earlier. The Kingdom itself comes only by the grace of God, and we can live the kingdom life only by God's grace. The first beatitude in Jesus' sermon that proclaimed the Kingdom clearly taught that the kingdom life begins and continues by grace (Matthew 5:3).

Chapter 1
The Kingdom Is Coming

The Vision of the Kingdom in the Old Testament

1. In this book we will be using the expression "Kingdom of God" as it is used in the New Testament: something that is not seen among men and then it arrives. It comes, and then it comes with power. This is consistent with Jewish thought and expectations in the first century. Of course, in another sense, the Kingdom of God has always been and always will be, for God the King has always been on his throne and the one who reigns over heaven and earth. But we use the term here, as Jesus did, to refer to the reign of God that breaks into man's history and to that which man experiences in a special way.

2. For a lengthy and thorough discussion of how the concept of the Kingdom of God is developed in the Old Testament, see

the classic work by John Bright, *The Kingdom of God* (Nashville: Abingdon, 1953), 17–186.

3. This idea has been developed in detail in the massive volume, *Jesus and the Victory of God* by N.T. Wright (Minneapolis: Fortress, 1996) and is a theme found in most of the works by the prolific Wright.

4. Bright, 116–117.

5. Shane Claiborne and Chris Haw, *Jesus for President: Politics for Ordinary Radicals* (Grand Rapids: Zondervan, 2008), 91.

6. Bright, 153.

Chapter 2
The Kingdom Is Here—Part One

Jesus and the Gospel of the Kingdom

1. Wilhelm Wrede used the term "messianic secret" but in referring to something entirely different.

2. The arrival of the future in the present age and the beginning of eternal life in this age is what the scholars refer to as "realized eschatology" or more accurately as "inaugurated eschatology." Eschatology, which comes from the Greek word meaning "last" or "last things," has to do with what happens at the end. Jesus' teaching is that the things from the end have broken into the present and are visible in some form now—thus the idea that the new age has been inaugurated and can be shared in, though it has not yet come fully.

3. For a clear and inspiring statement showing the balance we must keep between the *now* and the *not yet*, read Paul's words in 2 Corinthians 4–5. His vision of the age to come fuels his passion to be living a kingdom life in the here and now.

4. Thomas Jones, *No One Like Him* (Spring Hill, TN: DPI, 2001), 82. This is where Tom first proposed the idea that we should view the Kingdom as coming in waves.

5. John Howard Yoder, *The Politics of Jesus* (Grand Rapids: Eerdmans, 1972), 61.

6. Yoder, 114.

7. When the parallel passages of Mark 8:38–9:1, Matthew 16:28, and Luke 9:26–27 are looked at together, it may seem at first glance that they are referring to Jesus' second coming because of the words "coming in his father's glory with the holy angels." However, in John 12:23–26 Jesus clearly associates the Father's glorification of the Son with the "seed that falls into the ground and dies" referring in context to the death that he is ready to die. Romans 6:4 and 1 Peter 1:21 both connect the resurrection to the demonstration of God's glory.

But what about "with the holy angels"? Matthew 28:2–5 and Luke 22:43 and 24:23 together describe angels involved with Jesus both at the cross and in the resurrection. By saying, as all three Gospels report, "Some of you standing here will not taste death before..." Jesus is describing events that would occur in their lifetime. By the time the cross and the resurrection took place, one of the apostles, of course, had "tasted death," but most were living to see both the awesome display of kingdom love and divine power.

It would seem, then, that we must interpret Jesus' statement recorded in the synoptic Gospels either as a reference to the coming of the Spirit and the church on Pentecost, as was done in the tradition we both came from, or to the breaking in of the big kingdom wave in the cross and the resurrection. There do not seem to be other options. The former seems fraught with problems; the latter seems to fit all we have seen about the

Kingdom from the Old Testament forward, complete with the interesting twist that God often gives to man's own messianic expectations.

Finally, the cross and the resurrection as the fulfillment of Mark 9:1 fits with the idea of *prolepsis*, which means the representation of something in the future as if it already existed or had occurred. In the cross and resurrection, the end of the age occurs proleptically in Jesus. The future has broken into the present. That is the biblical concept of the Kingdom and a major theme of this book. At the end of the age Jesus will come in the Father's glory with the holy angels (Matthew 25:31), but in the resurrection that ending has broken into the present, so that we have tasted the powers of the coming age (Hebrews 6:5).

8. Bright, 170.

9. Young's Literal Translation renders the passage this way: "Wherefore, a kingdom that cannot be shaken receiving, may we have grace, through which we may serve God well-pleasingly, with reverence and religious fear...." The King James Version has the awkward but almost literal "Wherefore we receiving a kingdom...." Most English translations make an effort to capture the sense of a continual receiving, though it is not as clearly seen in the New American Standard which renders it as "Therefore, since we receive a kingdom...." Even there the translators avoid the use of the past tense.

Chapter 3
The Kingdom Is Here—Part Two

Jesus and the Gospel of the Kingdom

1. Ed Anton's excellent book on this topic, *Repentance: A Cosmic Shift of Mind and Heart* (Spring Hill, TN: DPI, 2006), gives many new and practical insights.

2. It was on the blog of Lee Hemen of Vancouver, WA, that we first saw a reference to the fictional country and its application to how we create our own kingdoms. His website is found at http://pastorblastor.wordpress.com.

3. For one example see Justin Martyr, *First Apology*, Chapter 61—"Christian Baptism."

4. G.R. Beasley-Murray, *Baptism in the New Testament* (Grand Rapids: Eerdmans, 1962), 231. The scholar-author advocates a return to the biblical understanding, role and practice of baptism in his 422-page work.

5. Beasley-Murray, 232.

6. Craig Watts, *Disciple of Peace: Alexander Campbell on Pacifism, Violence and the State* (Indianapolis: Doulous Christou Press, 2005), 126.

7. One of the most disturbing outcomes with this evangelical trend is that it leads to an attitude so accepted in the world that "the end justifies the means." An example: It is okay to use some violence if in the process we bring about a safer community. But we must say, "Not so with us." The means matter and Christians can use no means that are inconsistent with kingdom principles regardless of the perceived outcome. When we employ the means of the Kingdom, we can trust God to provide the end he wants, when he wants to provide it.

8. Alfred Lloyd Tennyson, "The Charge of the Light Brigade," 1854.

9. Various branches of what is sometimes called "The Restoration Movement in America," (aka The Stone-Campbell Movement) can trace this idea back to that movement's most famous personality and most articulate and influential writer, Alexander Campbell. On the whole, Campbell's works show commonality

with many of the things we are describing in this book, but he very narrowly viewed the church as being the Kingdom of God. That was the prevailing view in the group known as Churches of Christ, at least until recently. While this is true, two of the movement's more well-known personalities—David Lipscomb and James Harding—both whom have schools named for them, had a view of the Kingdom much more like we have presented, but nonetheless a view that was not widely accepted. On this subject we would recommend the book *Kingdom Come* by Hicks and Ballentine (see the bibliography).

10. We are in debt to George Eldon Ladd for this paradigm of thinking about the church and the Kingdom. He actually has five points not three, and the way he develops this can be found in *Theology of the New Testament* (Grand Rapids: Eerdmans), 105–119.

11. In our next volume, *The Kingdom of God Part 2: The Sermon and the Life*, we will devote our energy to examining "The Sermon on the Kingdom," beginning with the eight crucial Beatitudes.

12. Jones, *No One Like Him,* 111.

13. For much more on this see our book *One Another: Transformational Relationships in the Body of Christ* (Spring Hill, TN: DPI, 2008).

Chapter 4
The Kingdom Is Now—Part One

Today's Church Living the Kingdom Life

1. Thomas Jones, *God's Perfect Plan for Imperfect People* (Spring Hill, TN: DPI, 2001), 128–129.

2. Camp, 107.

3. Stanley Hauweras, *Resident Aliens* (Nashville: Abingdon, 1989), 74.

4. Claiborne and Haw, 137.

5. Camp, 153.

Chapter 5
The Kingdom Is Now—Part Two
Today's Church Living the Kingdom Life

1. This translation, originally done in 1961, was replaced in 1989 by the *Revised English Bible.*

2. Again we encourage you to see our book *One Another.*

3. Hauweras, 52.

Chapter 6
The Kingdom Is Not Yet
The New Heaven and New Earth

1. It is beyond the scope of this book to address the broader question of what happens after we die and the biblical teaching on the matter of paradise or the intermediate state, but see appendix 2 for a summary of this issue.

2. The term "oversoul" may have been coined by American thinker Ralph Waldo Emerson, but the concept came from Plato.

3. Isabelle Peretz, "The Nature of Music from a Biological Perspective." Available in PDF by entering the title in a search engine on the Internet.

4. Henry Kriete, *Worship the King* (Spring Hill, TN: DPI, 2000), 194.

5. Kriete, 199.

6. N.T. Wright, *Surprised by Hope: Rethinking Heaven, the Resurrection and the Mission of the Church* (New York: Harper Collins, 2008), 115.

7. Wright, 116.

8. Certainly in reading Revelation we have the issue of apocalyptic language that is not always to be taken literally. While there may or may not be a literal new Jerusalem, there is surely no doubt that John's message is that God is coming "down" to be with his people on the new earth.

9. Eugene Peterson, *A Long Obedience in the Same Direction* (Downers Grove, IL: IVP, 2006).

10. Mark 1:15

11. Luke 12:32

12. Matthew 13:44

13. Matthew 6:33

14. Mark 10:28–31

15. 1 Peter 2:21–24

16. 1 Peter 3:21–22

17. 1 Peter 1:22–23

18. 1 Peter 2:9–12

19. Hebrews 6:4–5

20. 1 Peter 1:13

21. 2 Peter 3:11–12a

22. Hebrews 12:28–29

23. Revelation 21:1–4

SELECTED BIBLIOGRAPHY

Anton, Edward. *Repentance: A Cosmic Shift of Mind and Heart.* Spring Hill, TN: DPI, 2006.

Beasley-Murray, G.R. *Baptism in the New Testament.* Grand Rapids: Eerdmans, 1962.

Bercot, David. *The Kingdom that Turned the World Upside Down.* Amberson, PA: Scroll, 2008.

Bright, John. *The Kingdom of God.* Nashville: Abingdon, 1953.

Camp, Lee. *Mere Discipleship: Radical Christianity in a Rebellious World.* Grand Rapids: Brazos/Baker, 2003.

Claiborne, Shane and Chris Haw. *Jesus for President: Politics for Ordinary Radicals.* Grand Rapids: Zondervan, 2008.

Hicks, John Mark and Bobby Ballentine. *Kingdom Come.* Abilene: Leafwood Publishers, 2006.

Hauweras, Stanley. *Resident Aliens.* Nashville: Abingdon, 1989.

Kriete, Henry. *Worship the King.* Spring Hill, TN: DPI, 2000.

Jones, Thomas and Steve Brown. *One Another: Transformational Relationships in the Body of Christ*. Spring Hill, TN: DPI, 2008.

Jones, Thomas, *God's Perfect Plan for Imperfect People: The Message of Ephesians*. Spring Hill, TN: DPI, 2001.

—. *No One Like Him: Jesus and His Message*. Spring Hill, TN: DPI, 2002.

Ladd, George Eldon, *Theology of the New Testament*. Grand Rapids: Eerdmans, 1974.

Watts, Craig. *Disciple of Peace: Alexander Campbell on Pacifism, Violence and the State*. Indianapolis: Doulous Christou Press, 2005.

Wright, N.T. *Jesus and the Victory of God*. Minneapolis: Fortress Press, 1996.

—. *Surprised by Hope: Rethinking Heaven, the Resurrection and the Mission of the Church*. New York: Harper Collins, 2008.

—. *The Challenge of Jesus*. Downers Grove: IVP, 1999.

Yoder, John Howard. *The Politics of Jesus*. Grand Rapids: Eerdmans, 1974.

AN INTERVIEW WITH THE AUTHORS, TOM JONES AND STEVE BROWN

DPI: When did you first begin to think some of these thoughts about the Kingdom of God?

Steve: I accepted the viewpoint that I learned in the congregation of the Church of Christ where I grew up. My thoughts were probably widened by the use of the term when we were part of the church in Boston. It was apparent that God was actively expanding the borders of his Kingdom, and the seriousness of the call to seek it first was invigorating to me, but this recent study has convicted me about how little I really understood about the Kingdom of God.

Tom: My graduate studies in theology put almost no emphasis on the Kingdom, but my major research project focused on a respected German theologian who, remarkably, believed in the resurrection. He presented the thesis that the end of history occurred *proleptically* in the resurrection of Jesus. After finding out what *proleptically* meant, I was introduced to the idea of the future breaking in to the present. That would prepare me for a better understanding of the Kingdom. However, my journey really began in earnest several years later in 1974 when I read John Howard Yoder's *The Politics of Jesus*. Though there was much I did not understand as I struggled through his work, I did start seeing the Kingdom of God not in institutional terms but in revolutionary ethical terms.

Soon after that I read George Eldon Ladd's *Theology of the New Testament,* which begins with a long section on Jesus and the Kingdom. This helped me see the Kingdom as so much more than the church, but very much linked with it. I was teaching Introduction to the New Testament at the time in the department of religion at Missouri State University and was energized in teaching the Kingdom concepts to my students. I soon put together a class on the work of Jesus with the Kingdom as a central concept. Most of that material would be published twenty-five years later with the title *No One Like Him, Jesus and His Message*.

DPI: What caused you to begin your focused study two years ago?

Tom: I had wanted to read Lee Camp's book *Mere Discipleship* for some time. I was going to hear him speak in July 2008, and I wanted to read the book before hearing him. The book reawakened in me so many thoughts that I had back in the '70s, some of which I started to share in my book on Jesus in 2002. I was impressed with the bold way he laid out things that I had believed but had too lazily consigned to the pile we call "opinion matters." I encouraged Steve to read Lee's book, and that began a serious quest by the two of us to get back to kingdom theology.

Steve: Like Tom said, he read *Mere Discipleship* and encouraged me to read it. Lee's writing really resonated with me and kick-started a storm of reading and talking and preaching about the Kingdom.

DPI: Were others involved with you in this study and this journey?

Steve: Very soon Tom and I began to involve other staff members and elders in the Greater Nashville Church in our study. Frank Williams, who was our evangelist at the time, was most enthusiastic and began to put into practice in our staff interactions the kingdom principles we were learning. Dave Mundie, one of our elders, who has a PhD in engineering from Vanderbilt, was especially eager to get involved. Tom set up a private blog, and he and Dave and I posted frequently on it to share with each other new ideas and build on each other's thinking. It was exciting with new insights coming every week.

Tom: Other staff members, Damien Charley, Barry Holt, Tim Kidwell and Keith Davis also contributed ideas and were very supportive. And, of course, so were our wives who didn't immediately embrace all our conclusions but encouraged our quest. Eventually word trickled out about our study, and other members of the congregation began to ask questions and share ideas that helped refine our thinking.

Steve: And, let me add that we shared our work with other teachers in our fellowship of churches, getting input from Gordon Ferguson, Wyndham Shaw, Douglas Jacoby, Steve Staten and Steve Kinnard. A weekend seminar on "Patristics" was sponsored by AIM (a ministry training program) featuring David Bercot, who is well known for his books *Will the Real Heretics Please Stand Up?* and *The Kingdom that Turned the World Upside Down.* That event also played a role in fueling our interest.

DPI: What has been the most exciting aspect of this study for you, or what has it meant to you personally?

Steve: It was exciting seeing formerly random ideas fit together in a unified framework and beginning to grasp the depth and power of God's Kingdom. (Not that I've got it all!) For me there was a variety of ideas and experiences growing up in the church of Christ: the excitement of working side by side with a missionary, Robert Martin, in the Fiji Islands for two summers when I was in college, feeling like this was what Christianity was all about, preaching the gospel constantly and training men to do the same. I owe Robert a lot for who I am today. His passion and boldness was inspiring. I had a growing discontent with the way commitment to Jesus was often preached about but not practiced, or sometimes even ignored completely. Studying missions and then living and working in other countries changed the way I viewed everything. In the Crossroads Movement and later in Boston I saw people living out their faith daily like I had only experienced in spurts. Of course, there was the reexamination of our core convictions after a trauma in our fellowship of churches. For me this focus on the kingdom brought all of this into a unified perspective and made sense out of all these somewhat disconnected things.

It was also inspiring to go back and read Restoration Movement authors whose names and reputations I was familiar with and see how a hundred years ago they were teaching and living out some of these same concepts.

Tom: For me it was returning to something that had meant a great deal to me earlier, but this time with a much greater openness to how it needed to affect and change my life. Also, this time around as a sixty-two-year-old, I am much more willing to speak out on some issues that may not be popular as long I am convinced they are a part of Jesus' kingdom message. I have become convinced that we have dismissed as disputable or opinion matters some key kingdom principles that are inconvenient for us. We wouldn't think of doing that on some of our long-held beliefs, but elements of Jesus' kingdom message are just as clear and maybe even more central. I am further convinced God will work in powerful ways when we are focused on the kingdom way, which is not concerned with being effective but faithful.

DPI: What concepts have you found most personally challenging?

Steve: The most exciting idea was understanding that we are really "aliens from the future" and beginning to grasp what this entails. The most challenging on a personal level was to wrestle with my attitude toward possessions. And I am still really struggling with how to fully live that out.

Tom: I personally settled some of the issues about the Kingdom and its effect on patriotism, the military and non-resistance long ago. But now, I see the need to speak clearly and openly about these things. What I have not done nearly enough thinking about is how the kingdom relates to my material possessions, my attitudes toward radical generosity and making financial decisions that go against all conventional wisdom for the sake of the Kingdom. There is what I call a kind of "over the top" obedience in the Sermon on the Mount that is exciting to me but challenging! Growth in this area has been fulfilling, but I have miles to go before I sleep!

DPI: As you have been teaching this in different places both in and outside the US, what kinds of responses have you received?

Steve: Initially very positive, people have been very excited to "connect the dots." It makes sense. There have been a few strong negative reactions to certain issues or applications, especially in regard to some of Jesus' teaching in the Sermon on the Mount.

Tom: Overwhelmingly positive. People are eager to see the big picture of the Kingdom. At the same time, some aspects of the Kingdom that we have sadly neglected are a real struggle for some people. When it comes to some of those areas where Lee Camp says we have certain deep-rooted (but unbiblical) Christian reflexes, we see some people just wanting to avoid the issues. Of course, this has to change and leaders must lead the way. Avoidance of clear teachings of Jesus is not the way of the cross or the Kingdom.

DPI: What obstacles will have to be overcome for the church today to live the kingdom life?

Steve: The hardest thing is to move beyond the intellectual discussion and put it in action. Beyond that we have huge cultural and nationalistic expectations that run very much counter to kingdom expectations.

Tom: (1) We will have to decide that though some of us have been very serious—even radical—disciples, we must be open to letting the Kingdom come in new ways. The obstacle here would be thinking that we basically have our understanding of the Kingdom down, and we just need to practice what we have been teaching. (2) We must once again overcome our fear of rejection. The Kingdom is so counter-cultural. There will be strong reactions to it—when we practice it all. We must prepare to be aliens and strangers.

DPI: What is your vision for how this could affect the church in our time?

Steve: Living the kingdom life is what "church" is all about. Teaching about the Kingdom is not some extraneous "new teaching." It is all about following Jesus every day and submitting to God's will. Hopefully as we live it out, we can truly become all that God has planned for us to be and to achieve.

Tom: The more I study Jesus' call to repent and receive the Kingdom, the more I see that repentance was not first of all a call to make some moral changes, though that was involved. It was a call for the Jews to give up their agenda on how the Kingdom of God ought to look and be shaped, and to turn to Jesus and completely surrender to his agenda. The writings of N.T. Wright have been very helpful with this. I believe it is time for us all to sit down and completely reevaluate our agenda as a church, rigorously compare it to Jesus' kingdom agenda and realign our priorities and reshape our activities accordingly. Evangelism is something that must not stop, as it seems to among many who focus on certain aspects of the Kingdom, but the evangelistic message needs to involve much more about the Kingdom—particularly, how its message is good news for the poor. When I read our book again just before it went to press, I wished we had put much more emphasis on how the Kingdom calls us to be with the poor. You can expect that emphasis in a subsequent volume.

DPI: This is part one of a projected three-part series. What will the next two books be about?

Steve: We have been calling the Sermon on the Mount, "The Sermon on the Kingdom" because it is such a clear statement from Jesus about how the reign of God is to affect our lives. So we want to devote the entire second volume to the Sermon, many parts of which we have sadly ignored. In our congregation in Nashville, we did a weekend seminar on the Kingdom and then followed it with seventeen weeks of study on the Sermon on the Mount. It all fits together.

Tom: Then in volume three, which will be subtitled "Aliens and Strangers, a Light to the Nations," we want to explore various ways in which kingdom values clash with and surpass the values of this world. We want to look at how the distinctive life enables God's people to become that city set on a hill.

DPI: Do you have any final thoughts for us?

Steve: May God's Kingdom come in ever increasing depth in our hearts and in ever expanding breath as the good news of the Kingdom is spread around the world. May his will be done, right here and right now, starting with me, just exactly as it is done in heaven. That about sums it up.

Tom: I believe with these thoughts about the Kingdom we are getting a grip on God's plan that is deeper, more faithful to the historical context out of which it came, but at that same time even more relevant and exciting for today's church. Finally, I try not miss an opportunity to ask people to pray for me: Please pray that by the grace of God, I may keep seeking to understand the vastness of this Kingdom as long as I live, and know the freedom that comes from practicing what we learn. My last thought is a prayer that we will ever be learning more about the Kingdom, but always being humble about how much we still need to learn.